HERBAL TEA RECIPES

Crafting Delicious and Nutritious Herbal Blends:
A Recipe Guide

LUCY ABBOTT

Table of Contents

Introduction 1

Welcome and brief explanation of the benefits of herbal tea... 1

Importance of crafting your own herbal blends 4

Overview of the e-book content 7

Chapter I: Understanding Herbal Tea 12

What is herbal tea? 12

The history and cultural significance of herbal tea 19

Different types of herbal tea and their benefits 23

How to select and store herbal ingredients 26

Chapter II: Essential Tools and Ingredients 30

Overview of the essential tools needed for crafting
herbal tea.. 30

Guide to sourcing high-quality herbal ingredients.................. 33

Commonly used herbs and their properties 42

Other ingredients to enhance flavor and health benefits........ 45

Chapter III: Getting Started: Basic Herbal Tea Blends.................49

Simple herbal tea blends for beginners 49

Step-by-step instructions for preparing basic blends 52

Tips for proper brewing and steeping.................................... 56

Common troubleshooting and solutions............................ 60

Chapter IV: Exploring Flavors: Advanced Herbal Tea Blends 65

Introduction to advanced blending techniques 65

Recipes for unique flavor combinations using different
herbs 69

Pairing herbs for specific health benefits............................. 72

Experimenting with spices and other additives 75

Chapter V: Herbal Tea for Health and Wellness..................... 79

Overview of herbal teas for specific health conditions........... 79

Recipes for teas targeting digestion, sleep, stress relief, etc... 83

Understanding the potential side effects and precautions 85

Consulting with a healthcare professional when necessary 90

Chapter VI: Herbal Tea Beyond Drinking 98

Alternative uses for herbal teas (e.g., in cooking, beauty
routines) 98

Recipes for incorporating herbal teas into food and
desserts.. 101

DIY herbal tea-infused skincare and haircare products 104

Creative ideas for gifting herbal tea blends 108

Chapter VII: Embracing Sustainability and Ethical Practices 112

The importance of sourcing sustainable and organic herbs .. 112

Tips for growing your own herbal garden 116

Ethical considerations in herbal tea production 119

Supporting fair trade and eco-friendly practices 122

Conclusion **126**

Recap of the benefits and joys of crafting herbal tea blends 126

Encouragement to continue exploring and experimenting ... 128

Final thoughts and closing remarks 131

Introduction

Welcome and brief explanation of the benefits of herbal tea

Tea made from herbs, often called tisane, has a long history of consumption in a variety of cultures all over the world. Herbal tea, on the other hand, is not manufactured from the Camellia sinensis plant like traditional tea is. Instead, it is created from a variety of dried herbs, flowers, fruits, and spices. It provides a wonderful and soothing beverage alternative that not only delights the taste buds but also offers a variety of benefits to one's health. In this section, we are going to discuss the multiple benefits of incorporating herbal tea into our everyday life. These benefits range from the potential of herbal tea to strengthen the immune system and improve digestion to the ability of herbal tea to promote relaxation and reduce inflammation.

The high level of antioxidants that are found in herbal tea is one of the most beneficial aspects of this beverage. Antioxidants are compounds that help fight free radicals, which are molecules that are unstable and can damage our cells. Free radicals can be neutralized by antioxidants. Herbal teas, such as green tea, chamomile, and hibiscus, are filled with antioxidants, such as polyphenols, flavonoids, and catechins, which play an important part in the process of neutralizing damaging free radicals. Regular consumption of herbal tea may help to contribute to overall well-being by protecting the body from the damaging effects of oxidative stress and lowering the possibility of developing chronic diseases such as cardiovascular disease, cancer, and neurological disorders.

The digestive advantages of herbal teas have been recognized and celebrated for a very long time. A number of herbs have naturally occurring characteristics that make digestion easier, help relieve discomfort, and encourage the development of a healthy digestive system. For instance, peppermint tea is well-known for its ability to calm an upset stomach and alleviate the symptoms of indigestion, including bloating and gas. Ginger has been known to enhance digestion, reduce nausea, and lessen the symptoms of motion sickness, therefore ginger tea is another option that is frequently chosen. In addition to chamomile, fennel, and dandelion root, there are a variety of other herbal teas that can help improve digestion, reduce inflammation, and promote liver health.

In the hectic world that we live in today, making time for relaxation and activities that reduce stress is really necessary if we want to protect our health. Tea made from herbs is an all-natural and gentle method to relax and find some peace in the middle of the chaos. A number of medicinal plants, including chamomile, lavender, lemon balm, and passionflower, include calming characteristics that can assist in the alleviation of anxiety, the promotion of relaxation, and the enhancement of the quality of sleep. It is possible to build a soothing bedtime ritual by drinking a warm cup of herbal tea before going to sleep. This will help prepare both the body and the mind for a good night's sleep.

A strong immune system is necessary for warding off infections and preserving one's health to the highest possible level. Teas made from herbs can be an effective ally in our effort to strengthen our immunological defenses. Echinacea, elderberry, and ginseng are just a few examples of the medicinal plants that are well-known for their ability to stimulate the immune system. These herbs include bioactive compounds that help increase the body's defense mechanisms, improve the immunological response, and shorten the length of the severity of colds and the flu. A healthy immune system can benefit from regular consumption of herbal tea since it can provide an additional layer of defense and support.

Herbal tea can be a helpful complement to a healthy lifestyle, particularly for people who are trying to keep their weight under control. Studies have been conducted to investigate the possible weight control advantages of several herbal teas, including green tea, oolong tea, and others. Catechins and flavonoids are found in these teas, and research suggests that they may help boost metabolism, accelerate fat oxidation, and facilitate weight reduction. Even though drinking herbal tea on its own cannot take the place of a healthy diet and regular exercise, it can be used as an addition to a program for weight management because it is a calorie-free and more hydrating option to sugary beverages.

Chronic inflammation has been associated with a wide variety of health issues, some of which are arthritis, cardiovascular disease, and some forms of cancer. Because of the natural anti-inflammatory characteristics that herbal teas possess, consuming them regularly may help reduce inflammation throughout the body. In the case of turmeric tea, the active ingredient curcumin, which is known for its potent anti-inflammatory properties, is present. It has been discovered that Rooibos tea, which is made from the leaves of the Aspalathus linearis plant, has anti-inflammatory qualities as well. We can potentially reduce the risks connected with chronic inflammation if we make herbal teas with anti-inflammatory properties a regular part of our daily routines.

In conclusion, herbal tea has a variety of benefits, some of which go beyond the soothing qualities associated with its flavor and aroma. Herbal tea has gained popularity as a natural and holistic approach to boosting health and well-being. This is due to the fact that herbal tea is rich in antioxidants, and it also has the potential to promote digestion, decrease stress, boost immunity, assist with weight management, and fight inflammation. Incorporating herbal tea into our life can create an experience that is both invigorating and therapeutic. This is true whether herbal tea is used on a regular basis as a ritual or as a treatment for certain conditions. Prepare a cup of your preferred herbal blend, take a few sips as you relish the myriad of advantages it has to offer, and then repeat the process.

Importance of crafting your own herbal blends

There is a growing movement to revive the lost art of crafting and creating things from scratch in a society where pre-packaged and mass-produced goods dominate. People are rediscovering the pleasures and advantages of creating their own herbal blends as part of this movement, which also extends to the world of herbal tea. Making your own herbal blends is more than just combining herbs; it's a creative process that lets you customize the flavors, aromas, and health benefits to suit your personal tastes and requirements. This section will discuss the value of creating your own herbal concoctions, including the opportunity to control the quality of the materials, the freedom to personalize, and the connection to tradition and nature.

You have complete control over the quality of the components you use when creating your own herbal concoctions. Herbal teas sold in commercial packaging frequently have additives, fillers, and artificial tastes that might affect the tea's flavor and quality. You can make sure you're using high-quality, organic products by procuring your own herbs and botanicals. You have the choice to choose herbs that are cultivated in the best conditions, picked sustainably, and free of chemicals. This level of quality control guarantees that you are ingesting a pure and natural product that is consistent with your beliefs and preferences as well as improving the taste and potency of your herbal blends.

Making your own herbal concoctions gives you countless personalization options. By making your own blends, you may satisfy the tastes of each person, who has particular health requirements as well as distinctive taste preferences. To obtain the ideal balance of flavor and aroma, experiment with various herbs, spices, and botanicals, depending on whether you prefer a strong and powerful flavor or a delicate and floral infusion. Additionally, you can modify your blends to target particular health issues or enhance general wellbeing. For instance, if you're looking for a blend to help with digestion, you could include herbs with digestive qualities like fennel, ginger, and peppermint. With such a high level of personalization, you can make sure that your herbal concoctions will complement your own wellness and health objectives while also tasting delicious.

By creating your own herbal concoctions, you can strengthen your relationship with nature and access age-old knowledge that has been handed down through the years. Herbal medicines and tea preparations have been used for their medical and therapeutic properties by cultures all over the world throughout history. Making your own blends allows you to actively partake in this age-old tradition. You grow a deep respect for the natural world and its curative powers as you pick herbs, dry them, and carefully blend them. Working with herbs helps you stay connected to the natural world's cycles, the changing of the seasons, and the abundant resources of the natural world. It acts as a reminder of our reliance on nature and the knowledge that lies within.

Making your own herbal concoctions is an artistic endeavor that promotes creativity. It's similar to creating a unique piece of art to choose the herbs, experiment with different combinations, and adjust the proportions. You are free to use your creativity to produce blends that express your character, state of mind, and desired outcomes. Maybe you want to combine chamomile, lavender, and lemon balm to make a soothing blend for relaxation. Or perhaps you want a revitalizing concoction with herbs like ginseng, rosemary, and lemongrass for an energy boost. There are countless options, and by adding your own distinctive style, you may design a tea experience that is entirely unique to you.

Making your own herbal concoctions can be a thoughtful activity that promotes ritual and presence in daily life. Taking the time to participate in the process of blending herbs helps you stay in the present moment in a world full of distractions and hectic routines. Herb measuring, grinding, and combining become opportunities for reflection and awareness. You let go of outside tensions as you concentrate on the activity in hand and lose yourself in the sensory experience. A sense of attention and connection is facilitated by the scent of the herbs, the touch of the leaves, and the hues of the botanicals. Making your own herbal blends can also turn into a treasured ritual, whether it's a morning tea ceremony to get the day started or an evening routine to unwind and find consolation. These rituals can act as pillars in your daily schedule, bringing solace, stability, and intentionality.

Making your own herbal blends is more than just mixing herbs; it's a journey toward empowerment and transformation. You start along a journey of self-discovery and well-being by taking charge of the ingredients, customizing flavors and health benefits, connecting with nature and tradition, expressing your creativity, fostering mindfulness and ritual. You are not only nourishing your body but also your soul as you relish each sip of your expertly created blend. So embrace the art of making herbal tea, and allow your creativity and intuition to lead the way on this enriching and fruitful journey.

Overview of the e-book content

The e-book "Herbal Tea Recipes: Crafting Delicious and Nutritious Herbal Blends - A Recipe Guide" is a complete resource for tea enthusiasts and health-conscious individuals who wish to explore the world of herbal tea and learn how to create their own unique blends.

The book is titled "Herbal Tea Recipes: Crafting Delicious and Nutritious Herbal Blends- A Recipe Guide." This e-book focuses on the flavor, health advantages, and sustainable cultivation of tea while also introducing the art of tea crafting. It acts as a guide, providing readers with the information, resources, and motivation they need to go on a journey of brewing and appreciating herbal teas.

Chapter 1: Understanding Herbal Tea

The purpose of the first chapter is to provide an introduction to herbal tea to the readers, giving them a solid understanding of what herbal tea is and the cultural relevance of herbal tea. It examines the contrasts between traditional tea and herbal tea, focusing on the numerous herbs, flowers, fruits, and spices that are used to produce herbal blends. The reader will also gain an understanding of the cultural and historical significance of herbal tea in a variety of diverse societies from all over the world. The chapter comes to an end with a discussion on the various kinds of herbal tea and the specific advantages that each variety offers.

Chapter 2: Essential Tools and Ingredients

In Chapter 2, the reader is presented with an overview of the necessary tools and ingredients for the creation of herbal tea. This chapter gives an overview of the equipment that is required for preparing tea, such as thermometers, teapots, and tea infusers. In addition to that, it instructs readers on how to acquire herbal ingredients of a high quality while highlighting the significance of organic, sustainable, and fair trade alternatives. The reader will get an understanding of regularly used herbs and their qualities, which will enable them to make well-informed decisions regarding the ingredients that should go into their mixtures. The chapter also discusses many other ingredients, such as spices, dried fruits, and sweeteners, which, when added to herbal tea, can improve both the taste and the health benefits of the beverage.

Chapter 3: Getting Started: Basic Herbal Tea Blends

The third chapter is an introduction to the art of blending herbal teas and acts as a beginner's guide. For readers who are just getting started with making their own tea, it provides recipes that are easy to understand and follow. The creation of fundamental blends is broken down into a series of easy-to-follow steps, which ensures that readers fully understand the procedure. The various techniques for preparing herbal tea, such as infusion, decoction, and cold brewing, are discussed in detail in this chapter. In this chapter, you will find information on how to properly brew and steep beverages, as well as frequent troubleshooting scenarios and solutions to those problems. The reader will have a solid foundation by the time they reach the conclusion of this chapter in order to create herbal tea blends that are flavorful and satisfying.

Chapter 4: Exploring Flavors: Advanced Herbal Tea Blends

In Chapter 4, readers are urged to investigate more advanced ways for blending in order to develop herbal tea blends that are more intricate and unique. At the beginning of the chapter, the reader is presented with a variety of herbs and botanicals, each of which has a unique flavor and set of qualities. After that, it presents a collection of recipes that display various flavor combinations. This gives readers the opportunity to explore and figure out which flavor combinations they prefer. The art of combining herbs in order to achieve certain health advantages is also discussed in this chapter. Examples are given to show how various mixtures can be used to target digestion, relaxation, energy, and other benefits. In addition, the readers are urged to try their hand at experimenting with different spices and other ingredients in order to give their blends more depth and complexity.

Chapter 5: Herbal Tea for Health and Wellness

The benefits to one's health that can be derived from consuming herbal tea are discussed in depth in Chapter 5, along with the ways that particular blends can help one's overall health. This chapter presents an overview of herbal teas that are often used for specific health concerns, such as aiding digestion, promoting restful sleep, reducing stress, and providing support for the immune system. In this chapter, readers will find a number of recipes that have been crafted specifically to address these issues, as well as information on the potential adverse effects and safety measures related with the use of particular herbs. The necessity of utilizing herbal tea as a supplemental treatment for overall health and wellness is emphasized throughout this chapter, as well as the need to consult with medical specialists when appropriate.

Chapter 6: Herbal Tea Beyond Drinking

The scope of herbal tea is expanded beyond its traditional uses in chapter 6, which may be found in this e-book. Herbal infusions for the skin, herbal blends for culinary purposes, and herbal tea as a base for alcoholic and non-alcoholic beverages are some of the different uses and applications of herbal tea that are explored in this chapter. The readers will learn about the numerous applications of herbal tea and the ways in which drinking it can improve their lives in various ways besides simply serving as a soothing beverage.

Chapter 7: Embracing Sustainability and Ethical Practices

The relevance of ethical and environmentally responsible practices in the production of herbal tea is discussed in the final chapter of the e-book. It brings attention to the negative effects that the production of tea has on the surrounding environment and provides advice on how to responsibly source herbs. The readers will gain knowledge on fair trade certifications, sustainable harvesting procedures, and the importance of supporting local and organic producers. The chapter also includes a discussion of the advantages of cultivating herbs at home as well as instructions for establishing a herb garden that may provide a consistent supply of fresh ingredients.

The e-book "Herbal Tea Recipes: Crafting Delicious and Nutritious Herbal Blends - A Recipe Guide" offers tea enthusiasts a plethora of information and ideas, providing a detailed overview of the process of crafting herbal tea. This e-book takes readers on a voyage of discovery and creativity, guiding them through everything from the fundamentals of herbal tea to the creation of complex blends, the investigation of flavors, the promotion of health and wellness, and the embracement of sustainability. The readers of this e-book will be able to go on their own tea-crafting adventures with the knowledge and recipes that are provided in the e-book. They will be able to create unique blends that will pleasure their senses and feed their bodies. This e-book is a useful resource for upgrading your tea experience and embracing the art of herbal tea crafting. It does not matter if you are an a beginner or an experienced lover of tea; this e-book can help you do both.

Chapter I

Understanding Herbal Tea

What is herbal tea?

Tea has been a popular comforting and energizing beverage for centuries and across cultures. The world of tea offers a wide variety of possibilities to meet varied tastes and preferences, ranging from the delicate flavors of green tea to the potency of black tea. Herbal tea has a unique place in this wide tea environment. The category of tea known as herbal tea, often referred to as herbal infusion or tisane, is distinct from traditional tea varieties. In this section, we'll look at what herbal tea is, where it came from, the different kinds that are available, and its health advantages.

Infusing or steeping various herbs, flowers, fruits, spices, and other botanicals in hot water results in the beverage known as herbal tea. Herbal tea is not prepared from tea leaves like traditional tea, which is made from the Camellia sinensis plant. Instead, it is based on the tastes, scents, and healing qualities of different parts of plants. Due to this distinction, herbal tea is a popular caffeine-free and non-tea alternative for those looking for a calming, tasty beverage without the stimulant effects of caffeine.

The use of herbal infusions has a long history rooted in ancient civilizations and can be traced back thousands of years. The therapeutic benefits of plants have been appreciated by many cultures, and they have been included into traditional treatments and rituals. These cultures have included herbal tea because it offers comfort, fosters wellbeing, and treats particular health issues. The indigenous communities of the Americas, the Greeks, the Egyptians, and the Chinese all had their own distinctive herbal infusion techniques and knowledge.

Herbal infusions were employed in religious rituals and medicine in ancient Egypt. The medicinal benefits of plants like chamomile, mint, and hibiscus were recognized by the Egyptians, who used them to treat illnesses and induce relaxation. The Greeks also recognized the medicinal value of herbs and developed herbal concoctions to treat a variety of ailments. The man known as the father of medicine, Hippocrates, advocated the use of herbal infusions to promote health.

Herbal teas have been used in traditional Chinese medicine as a vital component of therapeutic procedures for thousands of years. Herbal teas were traditionally consumed in China because of the culture's strong emphasis on the idea that one's body should be in a state of equilibrium and harmony. Even today, the use of particular herbs and botanicals to address imbalances and promote well-being is widespread.

Indigenous communities across the Americas have a profound relationship with both the land and the plants on it that can be used for medical purposes. They have been employing local herbs to address physical, emotional, and spiritual needs for years, passing down knowledge of herbal infusions through the generations. Herbal teas have played a significant part in many civilizations, from the Native American usage of sage for purification rituals to the Amazonian tribes' use of medicinal plants for healing.

Herbal tea contains a wide variety of flavors, aromas, and health advantages due to its extensive ingredient list. Let's examine some of the most well-liked herbal tea varieties:

Because of its well-known calming and soothing effects, chamomile tea is a popular beverage for unwinding and encouraging better sleep. This herbal infusion, which is made from chamomile flowers, has an appealing scent and a flavor that is delicate and floral with hints of apple. Chamomile tea, which is frequently consumed before night, is thought to ease anxiety and stress and promote calmness.

The peppermint plant's leaves are used to make peppermint tea, which has a cooling and energizing effect. Peppermint tea has a potent minty flavor that arouses the senses and is well known for its capacity to support digestion, ease headaches, and deliver a cooling effect. It is a popular choice for individuals looking for an energizing and calming cup of tea because of its energizing aroma, which enhances the whole sensory experience.

Ginger root is a well-known element in herbal tea blends because of its warming and digestive effects. Ginger tea is highly regarded for its capacity to reduce nausea, calm upset stomachs, and strengthen the immune system. Its unique flavor profile and distinctive aroma are enhanced by its spicy, slightly sweet flavor. During the colder months, ginger tea is frequently used to ease discomfort and enhance overall well-being.

The South African native plant Aspalathus linearis is the source of Rooibos tea, which has a naturally sweet, nutty, and slightly vanilla flavor. This antioxidant-rich herbal infusion is popular for its relaxing effects and potential health advantages. Rooibos tea is an excellent option for people looking for a tasty and calming beverage because it is believed to be caffeine-free.

Hibiscus tea is a well-liked herbal infusion produced from hibiscus flowers and is distinguished by its vibrant red color and energizing flavor. It has a tangy and pleasant flavor in addition to being abundant with antioxidants. Hibiscus tea is said to help hydration and cardiovascular health. Many tea enthusiasts like it because of its distinctive flavor profile and potential health advantages.

Herbal tea made from lemon balm leaves is well recognized for its relaxing and mood-lifting properties. It is citrusy and refreshing. Lemon balm tea provides a beautiful fusion of flavor and aroma and is frequently used to lessen stress, encourage relaxation, and enhance cognitive function. Citrus notes produce a rejuvenating and invigorating experience, making it an excellent choice for people looking for mental clarity and tranquillity.

A flowering plant called echinacea is frequently included to herbal tea blends to boost immunity and treat cold and flu symptoms. Because of its slightly bitter flavor, echinacea tea is frequently blended with other herbs to create a more flavorful beverage. It is widely consumed during cold and flu season or to promote overall immune health because of its possible immune-boosting qualities.

The possible health advantages of herbal tea are one of its primary attractions. Herbal tea infusions made from a variety of herbs and plants provide a wide range of therapeutic benefits. The following is a list of some of the potential health benefits that are associated with the consumption of herbal tea:

For centuries, people have relied on the digestive benefits of herbal teas like chamomile, peppermint, and ginger. A healthy digestive system can be supported by chamomile tea's ability to reduce bloating, stomach discomfort, and indigestion. With its calming qualities, peppermint tea can help with digestive problems and relieve stomach discomfort. Ginger tea, which has a warming effect, promotes digestion, soothes upset stomachs, and reduces motion sickness.

Some herbal teas contain relaxing properties that might help with relaxation and better sleep. With its mild sedative effects, chamomile tea has long been used as a bedtime beverage to encourage relaxation and reduce stress. With its citrus flavor and uplifting properties, lemon balm tea can help you sleep better by reducing tension. These teas are perfect additions to evening rituals since they provide a calming and comforting feeling.

Teas made from herbs like echinacea and elderberry are thought to boost immunity and help the body fight off diseases and infections. During the cold and flu seasons, echinacea tea is frequently consumed to bolster the body's natural defenses because of its immune-boosting qualities. Elderberry tea, which is high in vitamins and antioxidants, maintains a healthy immune system generally and aids in the prevention of viral infections.

Antioxidants are included in rooibos and hibiscus herbal teas, among others. Antioxidants are essential for shielding the body from free radical damage, which can speed up aging and cause chronic diseases. With its vibrant hue and distinctive aroma, Rooibos tea is a great source of antioxidants that enhance overall health. With its tangy flavor and stunning crimson color, hibiscus tea is another antioxidant powerhouse that promotes cardiovascular health and hydrates the body.

Herbal tea is a beverage that helps people meet their daily hydration requirements while consuming fewer added sugars than other beverages. Herbal tea is a great substitute for sweetened beverages since it offers a tasty and energizing choice that satisfies thirst and encourages adequate hydration. People may hydrate themselves while discovering new flavors and blends due to the large selection of herbal teas available.

Lemon balm and lavender herbal teas, for example, have mood-enhancing qualities. With its citrusy and refreshing flavor, lemon balm tea helps to promote tranquility and lessen stress. With its calming aroma and ability to relax the body and mind, lavender tea can help reduce stress and encourage serenity. Incorporating these teas in daily routines helps promote emotional balance and enhance mental health.

Turmeric and ginger are two herbs that are used to make herbal teas and have anti-inflammatory qualities. Curcumin, a substance recognized for its anti-inflammatory properties, is a component found in turmeric tea, which gives it its bright golden color and earthy flavor. With its spicy and somewhat sweet flavor, ginger tea reduces inflammation and has health benefits for illnesses including arthritis. Regular consumption of these teas may help people feel less inflammation and associated discomfort.

Traditional tea varieties can be replaced with delicious and healthy herbal tea. Herbal tea offers a variety of caffeine-free choices to fit various preferences and health needs by utilizing the flavors, aromas, and therapeutic characteristics of herbs, flowers, fruits, and spices.

Each herbal tea has a unique set of advantages, from ginger's aid in digestion to chamomile's calming qualities. Herbal tea continues to enchant tea enthusiasts all over the world, whether it is consumed for its claimed health advantages, its soothing properties, or its delicious tastes. So, the next time you're looking for a tasty drink, give a cup of herbal tea a try and enjoy all the benefits nature has to offer.

The history and cultural significance of herbal tea

With its complex flavors and potential health advantages, herbal tea has a lengthy and fascinating history that crosses several nations and civilizations. Herbal tea has long been an important part of human society, from age-old treatments to beloved traditions. This section will examine the fascinating origins, development, and varied ways that herbal tea has been accepted by various cultures throughout history. It will also discuss the cultural significance of herbal tea.

Herbal tea has its origins in ancient civilizations that were aware of the therapeutic benefits of numerous plants and herbs. For their therapeutic properties, herbs like mint and chamomile were utilized in herbal infusions in ancient Egypt. The Chinese laid the groundwork for the skill of blending herbal teas by cultivating and creating therapeutic teas as early as 2700 BCE due to their extensive knowledge of herbal medicine. These early herbal blends were employed as nourishing elixirs to enhance general wellbeing in addition to their therapeutic qualities.

Herbal teas were an essential part of holistic treatment methods as civilizations developed and spread, giving rise to traditional medical systems. Ayurveda, which originated in India, placed a strong emphasis on the use of herbal teas to balance the body's energies and promote good health. Holy basil, ginger, and turmeric are a few examples of herbal elements used in Ayurvedic tea blends that each have unique therapeutic characteristics. Herbal tea was also given a lot of importance in Traditional Chinese medicine (TCM) as a way to bring equilibrium back to the body. TCM herbal teas, frequently made up of complex blends, were intended to treat certain health imbalances and increase overall vitality.

The growth of trade routes and intercultural exploration facilitated the sharing of herbal knowledge and ingredients, which resulted in the continent-wide dissemination of herbal tea traditions. For example, the Silk Road was a significant factor in bridging the gap between East and West, making possible the trade of medicinal plants, aromatic spices, and tea leaves. Mint, chamomile, and rose petals were among the herbs that traveled from the Middle East to

Europe as trade routes developed, enhancing these nations' herbal tea traditions.

Herbal tea started to gain popularity during the European Renaissance, both for its therapeutic benefits and as a delectable beverage. The aristocracy enjoyed drinking herbal infusions that were rich in flavor and aroma and were made with ingredients such as lavender, rosemary, and lemon verbena. These herbal infusions were popular at the time. Herbal teas gained in popularity as a result of the development of herb gardens and the publication of books with herbal recipes, giving them a status of sophistication and refinement.

Herbal tea had great cultural significance in East Asia, particularly in Japan and Korea, where it became a crucial component of rituals, ceremonies, and meditative activities. The Japanese art of tea ceremony, known as "chanoyu," places a strong emphasis on the appreciation of tea as a means of mindfulness and spiritual connection. Matcha, a herbal drink made from powdered green tea leaves, became a representation of peace and harmony. Similar to this, herbal beverages like jujube tea and ginger tea are popular in Korean tea culture as a way to promote inner harmony and relax the mind.

Herbal tea traditions started to spread to various parts of the world with the rise of European colonial powers. The global spread of herbal teas was significantly aided by the British in particular. Local herbal tea traditions were enhanced by the introduction of herbs like chamomile and peppermint to the British colonies in North America and the Caribbean. In addition, herbal teas from indigenous cultures, such yerba mate in South America, made their way into global marketplaces, adding to the rich variety of herbal tea variations that are now available.

Herbal tea has seen a rise in popularity recently as more people turn to natural and holistic methods of wellness. Growing interest in the therapeutic benefits of herbal teas and the discovery of novel blends are both results of the wellness popularity. Herbal tea has changed from being a common beverage option to a traditional remedy, with a focus on organic and sustainably sourced ingredients. The demand for herbal teas that help particular health issues, such stress reduction or digestive health, has also increased, which is further boosting the herbal tea market's growth.

Herbal tea's history and cultural significance are woven into a tapestry of flavors, traditions, and a deep respect for nature's bounties. Herbal tea has traveled with human civilization from its ancient roots in medicinal brews to its modern renaissance in the wellness movement, providing comfort, nourishment, and a connection to nature's healing qualities. As we enjoy a cup of herbal tea today, we continue the tradition of appreciating nature's gifts and taking advantage of the variety of flavors and potential health advantages that herbal teas have to offer.

Different types of herbal tea and their benefits

Herbal tea provides a pleasurable and calming beverage experience with its wide variety of flavors, aromas, and potential health benefits. Herbal teas, which are made from a variety of plants, herbs, and botanicals, have been valued for their therapeutic qualities by many cultures for centuries. We shall set off on a voyage through the world of herbal tea in this section, learning about its different types and the distinctive advantages they each offer. Each herbal tea variety provides its own unique flavor profile and potential health benefits, from relaxing chamomile to energizing peppermint.

Famous for its calming and unwinding qualities is chamomile tea. This chamomile tea, which is made from the plant's flowers, is frequently consumed before bed to encourage comfortable sleep. Chamomile includes compounds that could lessen tension and anxiety while fostering a peaceful state of mind. Additionally, it has anti-inflammatory effects that can ease muscle tension and improve stomach distress. Chamomile tea gives a soothing and peaceful way to relax with its delicate, floral flavor and mild apple-like notes.

The pleasant flavor and wealth of advantages of peppermint tea, which is made from the plant's leaves, make it a popular beverage. It is well known for its capacity to promote digestion, calm an upset stomach, and relieve signs like bloating and indigestion. Due to its relaxing and cooling properties, peppermint tea can also help with headaches and migraines. As a natural decongestant, peppermint's menthol makes it a great choice for alleviating respiratory problems. Peppermint tea is a popular option for a revitalizing beverage due to its energizing minty flavor and fragrant properties.

Ginger tea is a warming and energizing beverage made from the ginger plant's root. Ginger tea, which is well-known for its digestive advantages, helps reduce nausea, ease stomach discomfort, and encourage a healthy digestion. It possesses anti-inflammatory qualities that could help lessen inflammation and pain in the muscles. Due to its antimicrobial and antioxidant qualities, ginger tea is also thought to enhance immunological function. Ginger tea gives a comforting warmth to the palate with its distinct spicy and somewhat sweet flavor while offering a number of potential health advantages.

Aspalathus linearis, a South African native plant, produces the leaves that are used to make Rooibos tea, sometimes referred to as red bush tea. This herbal tea has no caffeine and a flavor that is naturally sweet and nutty, often with vanilla hints. Antioxidants found in Rooibos tea, such as aspalathin and quercetin, aid in the body's defense against free radicals and oxidative stress. Additionally, it is thought to help cardiovascular health, enhance blood circulation, and support glowing skin. Rooibos tea is becoming more and more well-liked around the world due to its tasty flavor and possible health benefits.

The vibrant flowers of the hibiscus plant are used to make hibiscus tea, which has a taygn flavor and a deep red color. Antioxidants like anthocyanins, which are abundant in this tart and refreshing tea, may help lower oxidative stress and inflammation in the body. Hibiscus tea is thought to enhance cardiovascular health by assisting in the reduction of cholesterol and blood pressure. Additionally, it is a natural diuretic that promotes kidney health and detoxification. Hibiscus tea presents a wonderful and energizing choice with its zesty flavor and potential health advantages.

A citrusy and uplifting experience is provided by lemon balm tea, which is made from the plant's leaves. Lemon balm tea, which has relaxing properties, can ease anxiety, encourage relaxation, and enhance the quality of sleep. It has been used for a long time to treat digestive problems, such as indigestion and bloating. Lemon balm tea is a popular beverage for people seeking mental clarity and emotional well-being since it may also improve cognitive performance and mood. Lemon balm tea is a refreshing and revitalizing option due to its flavorful brightness and aromatic properties.

The purple coneflower plant, from which echinacea tea is made, has been associated to immune support and cold treatment. This herbal tea is thought to boost the immune system, assisting the body in warding off diseases and infections. It is frequently used to speed recovery and lessen the intensity of cold and flu symptoms when they first appear. The mild bitterness of echinacea tea can be reduced by adding other herbs and ingredients for a more palatable flavor profile. Echinacea tea provides a natural approach to wellbeing with its potential immune-boosting qualities.

There are a variety of flavors and potential health advantages available in the broad and alluring world of herbal tea. Each herbal tea variety has its own unique charm and therapeutic capabilities, from the calming effects of chamomile to the energizing powers of peppermint. Herbal teas have a lot to offer, whether you're looking for calming effects, digestive aid, immune-boosting qualities, or simply a flavorful and refreshing beverage. Accept the richness of herbal tea and savor its extraordinary fusion of flavor, aroma, and potential health benefits.

How to select and store herbal ingredients

People who enjoy herbal tea are aware that choosing the right ingredients and ensuring their quality and freshness are essential to creating delightful and nourishing blends. The flavors, aromas, and therapeutic characteristics of herbal ingredients must be preserved, which requires careful selection and storage. In order to fully enjoy your herbs and make outstanding herbal tea blends, we will examine the best procedures for choosing and preserving herbal components in this section.

When choosing herbal ingredients for your tea blends, there are a number of things to carefully take into account. First, put quality first by choosing high-quality herbs and botanicals that have been correctly harvested and processed, are devoid of impurities, and are of the highest quality. Find reputable suppliers who have an emphasis on herbs that are grown organically, sustainably, and ethically.

The appearance of the herbs is very important in judging their quality and freshness. Pick herbs that are colorful, have healthy leaves or flowers, and have not displayed any withering or discoloration. To fully experience the flavor and potential health benefits of the herbs, freshness is essential.

The aroma of the herbs is another crucial component. Spend a moment breathing in the aroma of the herbs. They should have a distinctive scent that represents their active ingredients and essential oils. A potent, powerful aroma indicates freshness and potency.

Also take into account the herbs' place of origin, as different geographical areas may produce varying flavor profiles and levels of quality. For instance, lavender from Provence may differ from lavender from other places in terms of flavor and aroma.

Herbal ingredients must be properly stored to preserve their potency and freshness. To retain the flavors and shield the herbs from moisture, light, and air exposure, transfer the herbs to airtight containers, such as glass jars with tight-fitting lids or resealable bags.

Storage ought to be done in an area that's cool, dry, and out of the sun. The quality of the herbs can be diminished by excessive heat and light, which also accelerates the loss of flavor and healthy ingredients. Moisture should be avoided because it can make herbs lose their effectiveness and make them more prone to mold and deterioration. As the humidity in a refrigerator can be too high, avoid storing herbs there and make sure your storage place is dry.

It is crucial that you clearly label each container with the name of the herb and the date of purchase or harvest. You may monitor the freshness and shelf life of your herbal ingredients by following this procedure.

Like any other natural product, herbal ingredients have a limited shelf life. Even though dried herbs often have a longer shelf life than fresh herbs, it's still important to keep an eye on and change up your supply. It's crucial to check and abide by the expiration dates on herbs that have been commercially packaged. Please take note that expiration dates are only a reference and not a guarantee that the herbs are no longer effective. Use your senses to determine which herbs to reject if they no longer smell good or seem unappealing.

Examine your herbs' appearance, aroma, and flavor regularly. It could be time to change them if they seem dull, smell weak, or taste bland. For your herbal blends to have the best flavor and benefits, freshness is essential.

Use more established herbs before introducing new ones by employing the First-In-First-Out (FIFO) strategy. This helps you avoid wasting herbs and preserves the quality of your tea blends by ensuring that you use them up while they are still fresh and powerful.

Those who have access to fresh herbs may find that picking and drying them by hand is a satisfying experience. Herbs should be picked while at their best, which is typically early in the morning after the dew has dried but before the heat of the day. When the essential oils are at their highest concentration, they have the best flavor and scent.

To prevent bruising or harming the leaves or flowers, handle the herbs gently. This preserves their flavors and healthy ingredients.

Choose a drying technique that is appropriate for the given herb. The best way to air-dry some herbs is to hang them upside-down in a dry, well-ventilated place. Others might need to be dried in a low-temperature oven or a dehydrator. To get the best results from any herb, adhere to the recommended dosage.

Once they have been dried, you should store your home-harvested herbs in the same manner as you would herbs purchased from a store. To avoid mold or deterioration, make sure they are thoroughly dry before putting them in containers.

For herbal ingredients to retain their freshness, flavors, and health benefits, appropriate selection and storage are essential. Your herbal tea blends will be of the finest quality if you select high-quality herbs, store them in appropriate containers and settings, and pay attention to shelf life and rotation. The care and consideration you put into choosing and storing herbal ingredients will enhance your tea-making experience and enable you to enjoy the full range of flavors and potential health benefits that herbal teas have to offer, whether you purchase your herbs from reputable vendors or gather and dry them yourself.

Chapter II

Essential Tools and Ingredients

Overview of the essential tools needed for crafting herbal tea

Making herbal tea is a fun and fulfilling activity that enables people to make distinctive blends suited to their tastes and health requirements. Choosing the right tools is just as important as choosing the right ingredients. We will look at the necessary tools for preparing herbal tea in this section, from the most basic utensils to more advanced equipment that can improve the process. Tea enthusiasts can improve their skills and make wonderful herbal infusions by learning about and investing in these tools.

The best tools for steeping loose-leaf herbal tea are tea infusers. They can be found in a variety of shapes, such as fine mesh baskets, silicone tea bags, and stainless steel mesh balls. Individuals can use these devices to immerse the herbs in hot water while keeping them contained so that they can be removed without any difficulty. Because of their dependability and convenience, stainless steel mesh balls are popular. Reusable silicone tea bags are an environmentally beneficial choice, while fine mesh baskets are appropriate for holding greater amounts of tea.

On the other hand, tea strainers are necessary for eliminating larger herb particles or loose tea leaves from the brewed tea. They come in a variety of shapes and sizes, including handheld strainers in the shape of a conical cone and larger strainers in the shape of bowls that are designed to fit into tea pots or pitchers. Tea strained through a strainer is smooth and devoid of debris, improving the entire drinking experience.

Herbal tea should always be brewed in teapots or kettles. Teapots, which are frequently composed of ceramic, glass, or cast iron, enable steeping more tea while maintaining heat. While cast iron teapots are renowned for their outstanding heat retention qualities, glass teapots have the visual attraction of allowing people to see the infusion process.

On the other hand, water is heated in tea kettles. With their quick heating, adjustable temperature controls, and automatic shut-off features, electric kettles are convenient. Stovetop kettles come in a variety of materials, including enamel, copper, and stainless steel, and they have a classic charm.

For herbal tea blends to have the proper flavor and strength, precise measuring of the herbs is essential. Kitchen scales, teaspoons, and other measuring devices help guarantee recipe consistency. Teaspoons and tablespoons make it easy to measure out small quantities of dry herbs; a leveled teaspoon is often equivalent to 2 to 3 grams of dried herbs. However, as different herbs have varied densities, it is advised to use a kitchen scale for exact quantities, particularly when experimenting with new recipes.

With the help of a mortar and pestle, people can crush and grind herbs to release their essential oils and enhance their flavors. When working with dried or harder plants, roots, or spices, this traditional tool is especially helpful. A sturdy mortar and pestle, such as one constructed of granite or porcelain, will provide durability when grinding. Herbs are kept as fresh and flavorful as possible by being ground right before brewing.

To keep herbal ingredients fresh and potent, proper storage is crucial. Herbs are shielded from moisture, light, and air exposure by tea tins or other storage containers with airtight lids. Light can be blocked and the herbs' quality can be maintained in containers made of non-reactive materials like stainless steel or opaque glass. Tracking freshness and shelf life is made easier by labeling the containers with the name of the herb and the date of purchase or harvest.

The experience of making tea can be improved by using some optional equipment, though it is not essential. Individuals can heat water to particular degrees ideal for various herbal tea varieties using electric tea kettles with adjustable temperature settings, assuring the best flavor extraction. Tea thermometers help achieve the ideal water temperature for particular herbs through precise temperature control. Digital or mechanical tea timers can help herbal teas steep for the right amount of time, eliminating over- or under-extraction.

Herbal tea crafting is a beautiful blend of art and science that calls for high-quality ingredients and the appropriate equipment. The basis of a well-equipped tea-making experience is built around the necessary tools covered in this essay, which include tea infusers, tea strainers, teapots, tea kettles, measuring tools, a mortar and pestle, and storage containers. Tea enthusiasts can improve their abilities, guarantee consistency in flavor and strength, and thoroughly enjoy the process of creating fine herbal tea blends by investing in these tools and taking care of them. Having the correct tools will improve your ability to discover the many flavors and health advantages that herbal tea has to offer, whether you are a novice or a seasoned tea enthusiast.

Guide to sourcing high-quality herbal ingredients

The process of crafting herbal tea is enjoyable and health-conscious, and it starts with choosing high-quality herbal ingredients. The flavor, aroma, and medicinal benefits of the tea are greatly influenced by the quality of the herbs utilized. The best herbal ingredients to use in your tea blends will be covered in detail in this section. This section seeks to equip tea enthusiasts with the skills required to produce delightful herbal teas, from understanding the significance of sourcing to investigating reputable suppliers and looking at quality indicators.

For a number of reasons, it is essential to source high-quality herbal ingredients. First of all, it guarantees the potency and effectiveness of the tea's health advantages. Fresh, high-quality herbs have a higher concentration of active ingredients that contribute to their therapeutic characteristics, like antioxidants and essential oils. You can trust on the quality of herbs and the beneficial effects they may have on your health if they are purchased from reputable suppliers.

Second, high-quality herbs have better flavor and scent, which improves the experience of drinking tea as a whole. The carefully chosen herbs have distinctive, vibrant flavors that can take you to several sensory landscapes. Your tea blends become more enticing and enjoyable due to the scents that come from carefully chosen herbs.

Finally, herbs that are produced ethically and sustainably promote ethical farming methods and protect biodiversity. You may improve the environment and the communities engaged in herb growing by choosing vendors who place a high priority on sustainability and fair trade. This thoughtful approach guarantees the survival of herbal traditions and promotes a more sustainable future for tea enthusiasts around the world.

The importance of obtaining high-quality ingredients cannot be overstated when making herbal tea. The flavor, aroma, and overall quality of your tea blends will be largely influenced by the herbs you select. Here are some of the options you have for locating trustworthy herbal ingredient suppliers. We will explore the many options available to tea enthusiasts to ensure the best herbs for their tea-making activities, from connecting with local herbalists and farmers to exploring specialty tea shops and online retailers.

Connecting with local herbalists and farmers is one of the most rewarding ways to find high-quality herbal ingredients. These individuals have a strong interest in herbs and frequently possess extensive knowledge of how to grow and harvest them. You may learn more about the complete process, from seed to cup, by developing a direct relationship with local suppliers. This tailored experience not only ensures uniqueness and freshness, but also enables you to support local businesses and strengthen the local economy.

Local farmers and herbalists are important sources for learning about the special qualities of various herbs and how to make use of them. Their knowledge can help you choose the ideal herbs for particular goals, such as enhancing digestion, encouraging relaxation, or increasing immunity. Furthermore, they might provide workshops or instructional sessions that will help you expand your understanding of and enjoyment for herbal teas.

Specialty tea shops are yet another great place to find high-quality herbal ingredients. These businesses place a high priority on choosing premium herbs and blends, sourcing from reliable vendors who share their dedication to excellence. Specialty tea shops frequently have knowledgeable employees on hand to offer advice on the different herbs that are available, their flavor profiles, and any potential health advantages.

Take advantage of the opportunity to have a conversation with the employees when you visit a specialty tea shop. Depending on your tastes and unique requirements, they might impart their knowledge and suggest particular herbs. Their suggestions could go beyond specific herbs because they can help you develop gentle blends that are tailored to your taste preferences and intended health advantages.

You can frequently find a broad variety of herbs in specialty tea shops, including rare and exotic varieties that might be difficult to get elsewhere. These shops frequently place an emphasis on freshness and provide herbs that have been meticulously picked and preserved in order to maintain their best quality. Discovering new herbs and enhancing your tea-brewing skills can be made possible by exploring the shelves of a specialty tea shop.

Through online platforms devoted to herbal products and tea, the internet era has created fascinating new opportunities for accessing herbal ingredients. By letting you choose from a huge variety of herbs and have them delivered straight to your door, these businesses provide convenience. To verify the reliability and quality of the shop, it is crucial to exercise caution and do extensive research while purchasing herbs online.

To get started, conduct some research into the credibility of online retailers who sell herbal products. To determine their reliability and dedication to client pleasure, look for consumer feedback and comments. Positive reviews reveal a reliable retailer who constantly sends out high-quality herbs. Additionally, it is a good idea to see if the shop offers comprehensive information about their sourcing procedures, including the locations of the herbs and any certifications they may have.

A reputable online herbal retailer would place a high value on the purity and freshness of their products. Look for vendors who make the appropriate packaging investments to shield the herbs from exposure to moisture, light, and air. Transparent labeling that includes the name of the plant, its place of origin, and its harvest date shows a commitment to giving clients accurate information.

The flavor, aroma, and overall experience of making herbal tea are greatly influenced by the quality of the herbs you use. When acquiring herbal ingredients, it's important to take into account a variety of quality indications if you're an enthusiast of tea. As you evaluate the quality of herbs, keep in mind the following important aspects: organic certification, harvesting procedures, appearance and aroma, packaging and storage, and supplier transparency. You may choose wisely and guarantee the best herbs for your tea blends by being aware of these indicators.

When acquiring herbal ingredients, organic certification is one of the most important quality factors to take into account. Herbs produced organically are guaranteed to be free of dangerous pesticides, herbicides, and other chemicals. Look for herbs with certified organic labeling or find more about the cultivation methods used by the provider. Choosing organic herbs helps preserve the soil's fertility and the environment's equilibrium while also promoting greater health for customers.

Herbal harvesting techniques have a big impact on how well they turn out. Herbs that have been sustainably picked from their natural environments and used as wildcraft frequently have outstanding quality. These herbs provide distinctive flavors and significant medical effects as a result of the varied environments in which they grow. When purchasing cultivated herbs, look for vendors who use moral and environmentally friendly growing methods. These practices put the health of the plants first, have a low impact on the environment, and improve the overall quality of the herbs.

The quality of the herbs can be determined through visual examination. When evaluating herbs, search for vibrant colors, unblemished leaves or flowers, and a potent, distinctive aroma. Herbs with a poor aroma or a fading appearance may be of lower grade. Freshness is essential, and the way the herbs look and smell may tell you a lot about how healthy and potent they are. Choosing herbs with these smell and visual signals guarantees a pleasant cup of tea.

Herb quality is mostly dependent on how they are packed and stored. The herbs should be packed properly to prevent exposure to moisture, light, and air. Airtight seals and opaque materials are ideal. The name, place of origin, and harvest date of the plant should all be clearly labeled on good packaging. You can evaluate the herbs' freshness and make educated decisions regarding their quality due to transparent packaging. Additionally, herbs kept in ideal conditions keep their potency, guaranteeing the preservation of their tastes and therapeutic characteristics.

Reliable vendors ought to be open and honest about their sourcing methods. They are happy to share details on the history, growing practices, and harvesting procedures of the herb. Suppliers with a focus on fair trade, sustainability, and ethical sourcing are frequently more reliable. Open communication with suppliers and relevant inquiries about their goods might reveal information about their dedication to quality. Suppliers who are open to answering questions and addressing your problems show their commitment to provide premium herbs.

To maintain the quality and integrity of the herbs used in herbal tea blends, it is essential to choose trustworthy suppliers. Finding reputable providers might be difficult due to the abundance of possibilities. Performing research and reading reviews, obtaining sample orders, establishing effective communication, and taking into account long-term partnerships are some of the key recommendations for selecting suppliers. Following these recommendations will help tea enthusiasts confidently select vendors who offer premium herbs, resulting in a satisfying tea-brewing experience.

An important initial step in evaluating suppliers is doing extensive research. Start by browsing websites and discussion boards with a focus on herbal teas and ingredients. Look for testimonials, reviews, and comments from clients regarding the goods and services that prospective vendors provide. Reputable suppliers have a good reputation and many positive ratings. Pay attention to previous customers' reviews who have purchased herbs from the provider and take their advice into account. This research directs you toward reliable choices and helps you reduce the number of prospective vendors on your list.

It is recommended to ask for sample orders from various vendors before making larger commitments. You can evaluate the quality of the herbs directly through sampling. Before making a big investment, it gives the chance to assess the flavor, scent, and general quality of the herbs. You can make informed selections and choose the best alternative for your unique needs and tastes by comparing samples from multiple sources. Sampling additionally enables early detection of any potential problems, such as poor packaging or variable quality.

Open channels of communication with suppliers must be established in order to assess their dependability and dedication to quality. Talk to vendors and find out about their sourcing procedures, quality assurance procedures, and any certifications they may have. Reputable vendors will respond to your questions and provide thorough descriptions of their goods. Their eagerness to answer questions and handle your concerns reveals their commitment to offering premium herbs. A solid supplier-customer relationship is built on the foundation of effective communication, which also contributes to the development of trust.

Numerous advantages might result from establishing long-term partnerships with trustworthy suppliers. High-quality herb suppliers can be valuable allies in your quest to perfect the art of creating tea. By working together, you can build trust, get tailored recommendations, and perhaps get access to herbs that are only available in limited quantities. You might eventually be qualified for exclusive discounts or other special deals. Building lasting connections with vendors that share your enthusiasm for herbal teas promotes a feeling of community and results in an outcome that benefits both parties.

The basis for making great herbal teas is sourcing high-quality herbal ingredients. Tea enthusiasts can make sure their blends contain the best ingredients by recognizing the value of sourcing, investigating dependable vendors, and assessing quality indicators. People can enjoy the delicious flavors and aromas that herbal tea provides, support sustainable agricultural methods, and obtain herbs with improved therapeutic potential through responsible sourcing. Tea enthusiasts can set out on a quest to learn how to make truly great herbal teas with the help of this guide. Tea enthusiasts can improve their tea-drinking experience and benefit from the numerous benefits that herbal teas have to offer by emphasizing the quality of the herbal ingredients.

Commonly used herbs and their properties

Knowing the characteristics of frequently used herbs is crucial when creating herbal teas. Each plant has special qualities and characteristics that influence how it tastes, smells, and whether it has any health benefits. This scetion will examine a number of herbs that are frequently used in herbal tea blends, looking at their qualities and possible implications on human health. These herbs, which range from calming chamomile to energizing peppermint, contain a wealth of undiscovered natural wonders.

The calming effects of the mild and peaceful plant chamomile are well known. The chamomile plant's flowers are well known for helping people unwind, calm down, and sleep better. As part of sleep rituals, chamomile tea is frequently consumed in the evening since it provides a calming and pleasant atmosphere. For those who enjoy herbal tea and are looking for peace and tranquillity, it is a popular choice due to its delicate, flowery flavor with traces of apple and pleasant aroma.

A stimulating and energizing herb, peppermint awakens the senses. Its bright green leaves have a distinct minty flavor and powerful menthol fragrance. The benefits of peppermint tea include helping with digestion, reducing headaches, and cooling the body. It is the perfect option for anyone looking for a revitalizing and refreshing cup of herbal tea. Peppermint is a popular choice for morning or lunchtime intake because of its stimulating qualities, which provide a natural pick-me-up.

Ginger is recognized for its warming and digestive effects and has an unmistakably spicy and slightly sweet flavor. This versatile herb is frequently included in herbal tea blends to reduce nausea, calm upset stomachs, and encourage proper digestion. During the colder months, ginger tea is a popular beverage choice due to its potential immune-boosting properties. Ginger is a well-liked ingredient in many herbal tea recipes because of its distinct aroma and energizing flavor.

The citrusy and reviving qualities of lemon balm make it a popular herb. The tea made from the lemon balm plant's leaves has a mild lemon flavor and a delicate lemon scent. Because of its relaxing properties, this herb is highly valued and frequently used to lower stress, encourage relaxation, and enhance cognitive function. Lemon balm tea is a well-liked option for people looking for a calming and energizing experience, and it's frequently savored during self-care and mindfulness moments.

The herb nettle is well known for its nourishing qualities and is nutrient-rich. For its potential health advantages, this herbaceous plant has been utilized for generations. Nettle tea is a well-liked option for individuals looking for a natural nutrition boost because it is well-known for being filled with vitamins, minerals, and antioxidants. According to common belief, it supports healthy skin, fosters joint health, and improves general wellbeing. Nettle tea has a mild, earthy flavor that is frequently enhanced by the addition of other herbs.

A fragrant herb known for its relaxing and mood-lifting effects is lavender. Lavender plant flowers produce a tea with a calming scent and a delicate, floral flavor. In order to relieve tension, encourage relaxation, and support a calm state of mind, lavender tea is frequently consumed. It is a well-liked option for establishing a calm and serene ambiance during periods of relaxation or meditation. Lavender is an excellent addition to herbal tea blends due to its mild flavor and aromatic properties.

The herb echinacea is well known for perhaps enhancing the immune system. This vibrant and robust herb is said to strengthen the body's defense mechanisms and aid in the battle against infections and illnesses. In order to boost overall immune function, echinacea tea is frequently consumed during the cold and flu seasons or as a preventive measure. It is a well-liked option for individuals looking to boost their immune system organically because of its flavor, which has a bit of sweetness and an earthy undertone.

Exploring the qualities of frequently used herbs in herbal tea blends reveals how nature may be utilized to promote wellbeing and provide interesting sensory experiences. Each plant has a unique flavor, aroma, and possible health advantages, from the calming properties of chamomile to the energizing effects of peppermint. Tea enthusiasts can make customized blends that suit their unique requirements and tastes by learning about the qualities of various plants. We may nurture our bodies, connect with nature, and go on a sensory adventure by embracing the benefits of herbal tea. In order to appreciate the benefits that these frequently used herbs offer to our lives, make a cup of your favorite herbal tea.

Other ingredients to enhance flavor and health benefits

When creating blends of herbal tea, the addition of other ingredients can improve both the flavor profile and the potential health benefits of the finished product. These elements offer a variety of smells, flavors, and medicinal benefits. They range from fruits and spices to flowers and roots. We shall dig into the world of additional ingredients in this section in order to increase the flavor and health advantages of herbal tea. These additions, which range from zesty citrus fruits to fragrant herbs and immune-booster spices, offer a delicious richness to our teacups and improve our overall well-being.

Lemons, oranges, and grapefruits are just a few examples of citrus fruits that are renowned for their vibrant flavors and energizing aromas. Herbal tea blends get a rush of vitamin C and a tangy, refreshing flavor when citrus zest or slices are added. Citrus fruits have been recognized for having potential antioxidant capabilities that can enhance immune function and guard against oxidative stress. They give herbal teas a zesty twist that awakens the senses and offers an appealing combination of flavors.

Strawberries, blueberries, raspberries, and blackberries are just a few examples of the berries that give herbal tea blends a natural sweetness and brilliant color. These tasty fruits are not only delicious but also abundant in antioxidants, which aid in the body's defense against free radicals. The benefits of berries for heart health and potential anti-inflammatory effects are well-known. They provide a delicate sweetness and a pleasant burst of flavor to herbal tea, making it a treat for both the palate and the body.

Due to their warming qualities and capacity to enhance the flavor profile, spices have been employed in herbal tea blends for centuries. Cinnamon, ginger, cardamom, and cloves are a few of the spices that are frequently used in herbal tea. For instance, ginger gives tea a spicy and energizing kick, while cinnamon gives it a sweet and woody scent. These spices are frequently associated to potential digestive advantages, such as relieving stomach discomfort and fostering healthy digestion. Numerous spices are also thought to have anti-inflammatory and antioxidant effects. Their addition provides warmth, depth, and a variety of possible health advantages to herbal tea blends.

For centuries, flowers have been added to herbal teas for their aromatic properties, which add a calming and refined quality to the drinking experience. Lavender, rose petals, chamomile, and hibiscus are some of the common flowers used in herbal tea blends. With its calming aroma, lavender helps people feel calm and peaceful. Rose petals are thought to have potential mood-enhancing qualities and add a subtle flowery fragrance. The calming properties of chamomile are well known, and it has a mild flavor. Hibiscus flowers, which have a tangy and vibrant character, are full of antioxidants and good for the heart. In addition to enhancing the aroma and aesthetic appeal of herbal tea blends, adding flowers may also have a number of therapeutic benefits.

To provide tea blends more complex flavors and health advantages, extra herbs and leaves can be added in addition to the primary herbal ingredients. For instance, mint leaves give herbal teas a cooling and refreshing effect while also boosting flavor and assisting with digestion. Lemongrass gives a lemony and aromatic tone that encourages relaxation and may help with anxiety reduction. Rooibos leaves have a naturally sweet and nutty flavor and may have antioxidant effects. They are frequently used as a standalone herbal tea. These complementary herbs and leaves create a complex tapestry of flavors and improve the tea drinker's general wellbeing.

Herbal tea blends are frequently enhanced with honey, a natural sweetener made from bees. In addition to its flavor-enhancing abilities, honey may have calming effects on the throat and can help with cold and cough symptoms. It is crucial to remember that honey should only be added to herbal tea after it has slightly cooled off because too much heat can destroy the nutritious value of the honey. A natural and healthier substitute for refined sugar, honey helps to balance and enhance the tea-drinking experience.

The variety of flavor, aroma, and health advantages for herbal tea blends can be increased by using additional ingredients. Berries add sweetness and antioxidants to teas, while citrus fruits add zest and vitality. Flowers give elegance and aromatherapy, while spices bring warmth, complexity, as well as potential therapeutic properties. Herbs and leaves add complex tastes and medicinal qualities. The natural sweetness and calming properties of honey are added to the tea. Tea enthusiasts can create unique blends that suit their palates and have a variety of potential health advantages by combining these ingredients. So, let's embrace the art of creating herbal tea and discover the countless possibilities these additional ingredients provide our cups. Happy tea drinking, and here's to a wonderful and nourishing experience!

Chapter III

Getting Started:
Basic Herbal Tea Blends

Simple herbal tea blends for beginners

Herbal tea is a fun and versatile beverage with a variety of flavors, aromas, and potential health advantages. Simple blends are an excellent place to start for those new to the world of herbal teas. To generate harmonious flavors and expose beginners to the art of tea blending, these blends frequently combine a few essential ingredients. This section will examine a number of simple herbal tea blends that are ideal for novices, offering a fun and approachable introduction to the world of herbal tea.

Two common herbs, chamomile and mint, are highly regarded for their calming effects and delectable flavors. These two ingredients combined produce a soothing and energizing tea blend that is excellent for digestion and relaxation. The mint leaves lend a refreshing, energizing aroma, and the chamomile flowers give off a delicate, floral flavor. This blend is great for unwinding after a stressful day or using as a post-meal digestion help.

Consider mixing the zesty flavors of lemon and the warming spice of ginger for a vibrant and invigorating tea combination. This blend has a stimulating kick and a variety of potential health advantages. Ginger root lends a warming, spicy aroma, and lemon adds a bright, citrusy note. The mixture is well-known for its possible immune-boosting effects as well as its digestive benefits. Take this combination in the morning to get your day going or in the afternoon for a refreshing pick-me-up.

Any tea blend is made more serene and elegant by the addition of lavender and rose petals. This calming mixture has a soft, calming flavor and an appealing flowery scent. Lavender is well known for its possible stress-relieving properties, while rose petals are thought to improve mood. This blend is ideal for relaxing at night or as part of a self-care routine. Allow yourself to be carried away to a place of peace and tranquility by the flowery notes.

A revitalizing and energizing combination of peppermint and lemon balm elevates the senses and promotes general wellbeing. Lemon balm leaves produce a zesty and energizing scent, while peppermint leaves offer a cooling and minty flavor. This combination is well known for its possible digestive advantages as well as its relaxation-inducing properties. Enjoy this blend as a cooling iced tea in the summer or as a warming beverage in the winter.

Echinacea and elderberry can be combined to create a herbal drink that promotes immunological health. While elderberry is thought to have antioxidant and anti-inflammatory qualities, echinacea is well known for its possible immune-stimulating capabilities. Together, they produce a blend that may support immune system development and perhaps lessen cold and flu symptoms. When you're sick or during the winter, this combination is especially helpful.

Rooibos, a herbal tea that is inherently caffeine-free, makes a fantastic base for flavorful blends. The addition of cinnamon gives the tea a pleasant warmth and complexity. While cinnamon lends a sweet and spicy touch, Rooibos is inherently sweet and nutty and is high in antioxidants. This blend may be helpful for promoting heart health and supporting antioxidants in addition to being delicious.

Two herbs that are frequently utilized for their potential detoxifying and cleansing effects are nettle and dandelion. They can be combined to make a tea that promotes overall health and helps the body get rid of toxins. Nettle leaves lend a delicate, earthy flavor, while dandelion leaves have a slightly bitter taste. This blend can be used as a daily tonic to encourage a healthy lifestyle or as a part of a cleansing routine.

It can be thrilling and satisfying to start the path of creating herbal tea blends, especially for beginners. Novices can experience the flavors, aromas, and potential health advantages of herbal tea without getting overwhelmed by complex blends by using simple ones. There are numerous simple herbal tea blends to suit different tastes and requirements, whether one is looking for calming effects, energizing effects, immune support, or other particular advantages. Beginners can learn the basics of tea blending by starting with these simple blends and progressively expanding their range to include more complex and unique blends. So, choose your favorite herbs, try out different combinations, and take pleasure in learning about the benefits of herbal tea. A wonderful and nourishing herbal tea is prepared!

Step-by-step instructions for preparing basic blends

A delightful and creative way to customize your tea experience is to make your own herbal tea blends. You can create distinctive flavors, aromas, and perhaps even some health advantages by combining various plants. We'll go through step-by-step directions for making fundamental herbal tea blends in this section. Whether you are a novice or an expert tea enthusiasts, following these instructions will enable you to start blending tea and develop your own unique blends.

Step 1: Selecting the Base Herb

Choosing a base herb is the first step in blending a herbal tea. Your blend's character will be established by this herb, which will act as its base. Chamomile, peppermint, rooibos, and green tea are typical base herbs. Depending on your preferred flavor profile and personal preferences, pick the base herb. Chamomile or rooibos both make excellent blends for calming and soothing effects. Green tea or peppermint tea are both excellent options if you prefer a blend that is energizing and revitalizing.

Step 2: Choosing Complementary Herbs

It's time to choose complementary herbs to enhance the flavor and potential health benefits of your mix after you've chosen your base herb. Choose herbs that work well with your base herb by taking into account their flavor profiles and properties. If you decided to use chamomile as your basic herb, for instance, you can think about including lavender for a flowery note or lemon balm for a zesty twist. Try out several combinations to find the ideal balance.

Step 3: Evaluating Flavor Strength

The strength of each herb's flavor should be taken into account while blending herbs. While some herbs have a strong flavor, some have a more delicate one. The proportions should be changed in accordance with the potency of each herb. Use more of that herb if you want a combination with a dominating flavor. Make sure the ratios are adjusted for a more harmonious flavor. Remember that individual choice plays a big part, so feel free to experiment and adjust the ratios to suit your preferences.

Step 4: Preparing the Herbs

It is crucial to thoroughly prepare the herbs before blending them. Starting with your chosen proportions, measure out the desired amounts of each herb. Make sure that your herbs are pure and uncontaminated. Herbs that have been dried are ready to be mixed. However, if you're using fresh herbs, you might need to gently air dry them or use a dehydrator to dry them first. Herbs should be dried properly for the best flavor and longevity.

Step 5: Blending the Herbs

Now that your herbs have been prepared, it's time to begin blending. The herbs should be combined in a bowl and gently stirred. To achieve uniform distribution, use your hands or a spoon. As you blend, pay attention to the aroma and how the herbs are interacting. You can refine the blend and make any necessary modifications using this technique. Remember that blending is an artistic and intuitive process, so trust your intuition and try out various blendings.

Step 6: Storing the Blend

It's crucial to carefully store your herbal tea blend after you've made it in order to preserve its flavor and freshness. To protect the mixture from moisture, light, and air, transfer it into an airtight container, preferably one made of glass or ceramic. Put the blend's name and the date it was made on the label of the container. Keep the mix out of direct sunlight in a cool, dry location. The herbs' potency will be maintained through proper storage, allowing you to use your combination for a longer time.

Step 7: Brewing the Blend

It's time to brew your herbal tea blend so you can enjoy it. Boil some fresh water first, then let it cool a little. To a teapot or a tea infuser, add a teaspoon or tablespoon of the herbal blend. The stated steeping time, which is often between five to ten minutes, should be followed when adding boiling water to the herbs. Depending on whether you prefer a stronger or milder flavor, adjust the steeping time. Pour the tea into your preferred cup after straining it. Enjoy the delicious flavors and scents of your own herbal tea blend while you sit back and unwind.

Making your own herbal tea blends is a great way to experiment with different flavors and potential health benefits while also customizing your tea experience. You can confidently start your tea blending journey by carefully following these step-by-step instructions. Choose a foundation herb, select herbs which complement it, consider the strength of the flavors, prepare the herbs, combine them, store the blend appropriately, and brew it to perfection. You can hone your tea blending skills with experience and experimentation and make distinctive blends that suit your tastes. So gather your herbs, unleash your creativity, and relish the satisfaction of creating your own herbal tea blends. Cheers to a cup of healthy and delectable home-brewed herbal tea!

Tips for proper brewing and steeping

The process of brewing and steeping herbal tea is an art that requires careful attention to detail in addition to an understanding of the characteristics of the herbs. The flavor, aroma, and potential health benefits that can be derived from the herbs depend on the brewing procedure. In order to get the greatest results when brewing and steeping herbal tea, we will give you helpful advice in this section. These recommendations will enable you to improve your tea-drinking experience and get the most out of your herbal blends, regardless of your level of tea experience.

The flavor and aroma of the herbal tea are greatly influenced by the quality of the water used to prepare it. To ensure a clean and pure flavor, start with fresh, filtered water every time. Do not use tap water since it may contain chlorine or other impurities that will change the flavor of your tea. In order to extract the qualities of the herbs, the water's temperature is also very important. While tougher plants like peppermint or ginger can be steeped at boiling point, around 212°F (100°C), delicate herbs like chamomile or green tea require lower temperatures around 175°F (80°C).

For a cup of herbal tea to be well-rounded and tasty, the appropriate herb balance must be found. Use roughly one teaspoon of dry herbs or one tablespoon of fresh herbs per cup of water as a general rule. Depending on whether you prefer a stronger or softer brew, adjust the amount. To prevent overpowering the blend, keep in mind that some herbs may have stronger flavors and may require less quantities. Additionally, it's crucial to take the size of your teapot or infuser into account and adjust the amount appropriately to provide the herbs enough space to expand during steeping.

The right amount of steeping time is essential for getting the best flavor and scent out of the herbs. The length of time for steeping varies depending on the type of herb and preference. In order to avoid bitterness, delicate herbs like chamomile or lavender often need to steep for only 5 to 7 minutes. Longer steeping times, up to 10 minutes, may be necessary for stronger herbs like hibiscus or rosemary to fully extract their flavors. To get the ideal flavor without any undesirable bitterness or strong flavors, it is crucial to adhere to the suggested steeping time limits given for each herb.

The right brewing vessel must be used in order to produce a cup of herbal tea that is tasty and well-infused. Choose a teapot or tea infuser that enables the herbs to spread out and fully unleash their flavors. The flavors and qualities of the herbs are not harmed by using stainless steel infusers or tea bags produced from unbleached natural materials. Avoid using plastic or metal containers because they may change the flavor and impact how you experience tea overall.

To ensure a tasty and aromatic cup of herbal tea, cover the brewing vessel while steeping to maintain heat and prevent the evaporation of essential oils. While the tea is steeping, cover the teapot or cup with a lid or other covering to retain heat and let the herbs fully infuse. Additionally, this approach reduces any potential contamination from dust or other outside factors.

With herbal tea, you can play about with the infusion time to find new flavors and intensities. You can experiment by using the same herbs for shorter or longer infusion times, and then comparing the flavor characteristics. Shorter infusion times may result in a lighter and more delicate cup, while longer infusion times may extract more strong flavors and potential health benefits. The decision ultimately comes down to preference and the intended result.

Keep in mind that everyone has different tastes and interests. You can add a little hot water to the flavor to weaken it if you feel it to be too intense. On the other hand, if the flavor is too subtle, add more herbs or lengthen the steeping process. You can modify the brewing procedure to make the tea to your preferences by experimenting with it.

The flavors and aromas of herbal tea are best experienced immediately after brewing. Avoid letting the tea sit for too long because it could lose its freshness and flavor. Spend some time indulging in the sensory experience of the freshly brewed herbal tea to savor the moment.

Your herbal ingredients' longevity and quality are guaranteed by properly storing them. Herbs should be kept dry and free from moisture, strong odors, and direct sunlight in airtight containers. Their flavors and strength are preserved as a result. To avoid flavor and fragrance contamination, keep various herbs apart. Label each container with the herb's name and the date to keep track of its freshness.

Herbal tea brewing is a creative endeavor that encourages experimentation, customization, and creativity. Don't be afraid to experiment and develop your own distinctive blends as you gain expertise and knowledge about various herbs, flavors, and brewing methods. To improve your brewing abilities, interact with the tea community, go to workshops or tastings, and share ideas.

To get the most out of herbs and make a delicious cup of herbal tea, proper brewing and steeping methods are necessary. By implementing these suggestions, you can improve your tea-drinking experience and take advantage of the herbal mixes' complex flavors, scents, and health advantages. Make sure to embrace the art of tea brewing by using fresh, high-quality water, adjusting the amount of herbs, paying attention to the steeping time, choosing the right brewing vessel, covering and protecting while steeping, experimenting with infusion times, and adjusting for personal preference. Savor freshly brewed tea, store herbs properly, and use fresh, high-quality water. You may become an expert at making herbal tea with practice and exploration, and you'll learn how much pleasure it can bring. Cheers to a voyage full of energizing and delicious herbal teas!

Common troubleshooting and solutions

Making herbal tea is a delicate procedure that calls for accuracy and a touch of creativity. Even seasoned tea lovers, though, could run into difficulties along the way. Unexpected results, such as brittleness or weak flavors, can ruin the tea-drinking experience. In this section, we will examine the typical problems that arise when making herbal tea and offer workable strategies to troubleshoot and resolve these problems. You can improve your tea-making abilities and get the full rewards of tasty and aromatic herbal infusions by arming yourself with the information to handle these difficulties.

A bitter or excessively strong flavor in the herbal tea is one of the most typical problems. This might happen if herbs are steeped for a long period of time or are utilized in large quantities. It is crucial to concentrate on the steeping period and herb-to-water ratio in order to solve this issue.

Reduce the steeping time to lessen bitterness. Start with a lesser time frame—such, three to four minutes—and then experiment with it to suit your tastes. To achieve the ideal balance, it is also advisable to refer to the suggested steeping times for particular herbs. Alternatively, reduce the amount of herbs used or change the proportion of herbs to water. Start with a smaller quantity and build it up gradually until the desired flavor is obtained. To discover the ideal balance for your palate, experimenting may be required because each herb has a distinctive strength.

On the other hand, certain herbal teas could have a weak or subtle flavor and fall short of providing the required taste. Concentrate on the amount of herbs and steeping time to overcome this challenge.

Increase the steeping time a little to bring out the flavor. Add a minute or two to the suggested time frame and modify to suit your preferences. Finding the ideal steeping period that enables the herbs to release their full flavor without turning bitter is essential. Additionally, think about boosting the infusion's herb content. This adjustment may increase the flavor profile and produce a stronger flavor. Keep in mind that different herbs may require varying quantities for effective flavor extraction as you experiment by progressively adding more herbs until the desired flavor is attained.

An essential element of the total sensory experience is the aroma of herbal tea. It could be disappointing if the tea doesn't have a strong or noticeable aroma. Concentrate on herb freshness and steeping conditions to solve this problem.

Make sure the herbs are high-quality and fresh before anything else. Since the aroma fades with time, it's essential to buy fresh herbs from reputable vendors. The fragrant qualities of the herbs are preserved by careful storage in airtight containers that are kept dry, away from moisture, and strong odors. Next, think about modifying the steeping conditions to improve the aroma. While being careful not to go beyond and run the danger of producing a bitter flavor, gently increase the steeping duration or temperature. Discover the delicate balance that brings out the herbs' full fragrant potential by experimenting with various steeping settings.

If making herbal tea, consistency in flavor is a desirable quality. Nevertheless, accomplishing this might be difficult, particularly when using loose herbs or blends with different quantities. Concentrate on precise measures and pre-mixing blends to guarantee a consistent flavor profile.

To preserve consistency, using standardized measures for herbs is crucial. To correctly measure the herbs and guarantee a consistent flavor every time you brew, use teaspoons or tablespoons. For future usage, it's also a good idea to write down the precise herb ratios utilized in successful brews. Consider pre-mixing the herbs in a certain ratio before brewing if you're using herbal tea blends. This strategy eliminates the possibility of flavor differences brought on by uneven herb application and ensures a constant flavor profile throughout all cups. You can also modify blends to suit your preferences by pre-mixing.

When brewing loose herbs or blends, it's usual to notice herb sediment or residue in the bottom of the cup. Some people don't mind it, but others would rather have a smoother sipping experience. Consider using strainers or filters to reduce or remove herb residue.

Practical tools that assist in separating the herbs from the infused liquid include strainers and infuser baskets. These tools guarantee a clear and sediment-free tea by preventing herb particles from getting into the cup. Invest on fine-mesh strainers or infuser baskets that can trap tiny herb particles while yet allowing water to flow freely. Use disposable tea filters for a more sophisticated solution. These bags are porous and can be used to soak herbs like a tea bag. Tea filters offer another layer of filtration, producing an infusion that is clear and sediment-free. They make brewing convenient and hassle-free because they are simple to dispose of after use.

Herbal teas may have a bad aftertaste that takes away from how much you like the drink. Focus on modifying the steeping duration and making sure to utilize high-quality ingredients to solve this problem.

Reduce the steeping time to prevent over-extraction and a bad aftertaste. Long-term steeping may result in an unfavorable flavor. To get the best balance between flavor extraction and reducing any off flavors, experiment with shorter steeping times. Make sure the herbs are fresh and of excellent quality as well. Herbs that are of lower quality or that have been stored for a long time may have a higher chance of leaving a bad aftertaste. To improve the overall flavor, choose fresh herbs from trusted vendors.

Herbal tea's color can play a significant role in its attraction. It can be disappointing if the tea lacks vibrancy or doesn't have the desired hue. Concentrate on herb selection and changing herb quantities to solve this problem.

To improve the tea's aesthetic appeal, choose herbs with vibrant colors. Hibiscus flowers, for instance, can add a strong red tint, and butterfly pea flowers, a vivid blue one. Try out various herbs to make visually appealing and alluring beverages. In order to increase the color, you should also change the amount of herbs utilized. A richer and more saturated hue can be obtained by adding more herbs. Try varying the ratios until the correct color is obtained, but keep in mind that some herbs could need more of them to provide the intended result.

Learning the art of making herbal tea requires a thorough understanding of problem-solving techniques. You may overcome challenges and improve your tea-making abilities by being aware of typical problems and putting the right solutions into practice. Don't forget to experiment with steeping times, verify herb freshness, standardize measures, use strainers or filters, take aftertaste variables into consideration, and use herbs with vibrant hues. You can learn to properly troubleshoot and consistently make delicious and pleasant cups of herbal tea with practice and patience. Enjoy your exploration of the flavors, aromas, and healing properties of this traditional beverage. Let's celebrate the benefits of herbal tea!

Chapter IV

Exploring Flavors:
Advanced Herbal Tea Blends

Introduction to advanced blending techniques

Herbal tea comes in a wide variety of flavors and scents, each with special qualities and healing properties. While basic blending provides a strong basis, advanced blending methods raise the standard for the development of herbal teas. We will delve into the intricacies of advanced blending methods in this section, looking at the use of complementary flavors, balancing herbal profiles, and incorporating specialized ingredients to produce complex and harmonious tea blends. You will discover countless opportunities to create teas that satisfy the senses and nourish the body and spirit by exploring the world of expert blending.

The use of herbs and components that improve and complement one another's flavors is a component of advanced blending techniques. Tea blends with layered complexity and a well-rounded palate experience can be made by blending herbs with complementing flavor qualities.

Think about blending herbs with diverse flavor profiles. For instance, combining the earthy sweetness of licorice root with the bright and acidic tones of citrus herbs like lemongrass or lemon verbena can produce a pleasing balance. Similar to how relaxing herbs like lavender or rose petals can accentuate the flowery and delicate qualities of chamomile.

Try matching various types of herbs with each other to create new flavors, such as fruity and herbal roots or minty and spicy. You can make teas that exhibit a pleasing mix of flavors and offer a diverse taste experience by experimenting with these combinations.

It takes careful consideration of the unique qualities of each herb and developing a harmonious blend to make well-balanced herbal tea blends. Finding the ideal balance is crucial for a successful blend because each herb contributes its unique flavor, aroma, and medicinal properties.

Choose the primary herb or ingredient that will be the base of your blend first. Whether the tea's primary goal is to promote relaxation, immunological support, or digestive wellbeing, this herb should be the star of the show. Then, incorporate secondary herbs that deepen and add complexity to the primary herb's characteristics by enhancing and complementing them.

It's critical to consider how strongly each herb's flavor is expressed. If used in excess, some plants' stronger flavors can overpower those of other herbs. By adjusting the amount of each herb in the blend, you may balance the ratios of the herbs. This makes it possible for the flavors to combine smoothly and makes sure that no one herb dominates the entire flavor profile.

Advanced blending methods frequently entail the use of specific ingredients to provide tea blends depth, complexity, and distinctive qualities. These ingredients can broaden the palette of flavors and aromas in your creations by adding spices, botanicals, fruits, and even culinary herbs.

Spices like cinnamon, ginger, cardamom, and cloves can give tea blends a warm, rich, and somewhat spiciness. Create teas with a calming and energizing flavor by experimenting with various spice blends.

Tea blends can benefit from the vibrant hues, floral fragrances, and visual appeal that botanicals like elderflower, hibiscus petals, and butterfly pea flowers can add. They offer extra health advantages in addition to adding to the overall sensory experience.

Fruits can provide a natural sweetness and fruity undertones to tea blends, whether they are fresh or dried. Berries can give a delightful acidity, while citrus fruits like orange or lemon zest can add brightness. Dried fruit pieces, such as slices of apple or pineapple, can add sweetness and complexity to the blend naturally.

Herbal teas can be given surprising twists and unique flavor profiles by adding culinary herbs like basil, thyme, or rosemary. These herbs can give a simple tea blend depth and complexity, turning it into a culinary adventure.

Additionally, customization to target particular health benefits is possible with advanced blending techniques. You can make tea blends that target particular wellness objectives by combining herbs with complementary therapeutic effects.

Using herbs with relaxing effects like chamomile, lavender, and lemon balm, for instance, can help you make a blend that encourages rest and sleep. These herbs work together to produce a calming and peaceful combination.

Consider blending immune-supporting herbs like echinacea, elderberry, and ginger to improve immunological health. Together, these herbs strengthen the body's defenses and advance overall health.

Herbs with soothing and digestive properties including peppermint, fennel, and ginger can be included in blends for digestive well-being. These herbs can aid in promoting healthy digestion and easing digestive discomfort.

Understanding the characteristics of various herbs and how they interact is necessary to create blends that offer certain health benefits. You can create blends that support wellbeing and meet your individual needs by conducting research and trying out different combinations.

Advanced blending techniques increase the craft of making herbal tea and provide an expansive area for taste research and tea brewing. You may maximize the potential of herbal teas by understanding the concepts of complementary flavor pairings, balancing herbal profiles, combining specialized ingredients, and creating blends for health benefits.

A deep appreciation for the varied world of herbs and botanicals is encouraged along the journey of advanced blending. Take advantage of the opportunity to experiment with new blendings, develop your palate, and produce teas that delight the senses. You will go on a sensory journey with each cup that will nourish your body and spirit, enhancing your tea experience and providing joy to others who consume your exquisitely created herbal blends. Cheers to the science of advanced herbal tea blending!

Recipes for unique flavor combinations using different herbs

Tea enthusiasts can create distinctive and delectable blends of herbs, flowers, fruits, and spices through the practice of herbal tea blending, which is an art. We will explore several recipes for delightful herbal tea brews in this section, highlighting the variety of flavors and the virtually limitless blending options. These recipes, which range from calming floral blends to energizing and spicy infusions, will spark your creativity and motivate you to produce original works of art.

The delicate combination of chamomile flowers, lavender buds, and lemon verbena leaves makes up the Tranquil Garden Blend. Together, these relaxing components produce a quiet and fragrant infusion that encourages tranquility and relaxation. The mild calming qualities of chamomile are well recognized, and lavender adds a floral and aromatic touch. Lemon verbena adds a zesty taste that balances the blend and gives it a light twist.

The Berry Blast blend includes hibiscus petals, rosehips, elderberries, blueberries, and a hint of peppermint for a blast of fruity aromas. Elderberries and blueberries add a deep sweetness to the hibiscus and rosehips' acidic and sour flavors. A bright and energizing tea experience is created by adding peppermint leaves, which also lend a cooling touch.

The warming Spiced Citrus Infusion combines the powerful flavors of rooibos leaves with the zest of orange peel, the warmth of cinnamon sticks, and the aromatic hints of cardamom pods and cloves. The warming and well-balanced combination of citrus notes and spices in this blend makes it ideal for chilly winter days or cozy evenings.

A symphony of delicate and aromatic flowers create the Floral Delight blend. It creates a tea that is visually attractive and a treat for the senses by combining rose petals, jasmine flowers, calendula petals, and lemon balm leaves. Calendula petals' gentle sweetness enhances the floral aromas of roses and jasmine, while the uplifting and refreshing qualities of lemon balm leaves round out the composition.

The Energizing Ginger Zing combines the spiciness of ginger root with the citrusy tastes of lemongrass and lemon zest, as well as the cooling freshness of peppermint leaves, for a revitalizing and energizing blend. This mixture offers a zesty and invigorating sensation that is great for increasing energy and awaking the senses.

The recipes shown here are just a few examples of the countless options that herbal tea mixing provides. There are countless variants of wonderful and flavorful tea blends that you can make by experimenting with various herbs, flowers, fruits, and spices. Trusting your senses, experimenting with different pairings, and embracing your creativity are the keys to good blending.

Remember to start with high-quality ingredients and experiment with different ratios to get the ideal taste profiles as you set out on your own tea blending journey. Take note of each ingredient's distinctive qualities and how they work together. There are no set guidelines for blending herbal teas, which is one of their wonderful features. Instead, follow your instincts and personal preferences.

Learn to enjoy creating unique blends that are customized to match your preferences and moods. Accept the skill of blending herbal teas as a method to express oneself and an excellent way to enjoy the wonders of nature with each drink. Cheers to the discovery of flavor, the search for harmony, and the enjoyment of savoring a great cup of herbal tea.

Pairing herbs for specific health benefits

Herbs have been utilized as natural remedies for promoting health and well-being for centuries. Each herb has special qualities that can support a range of health advantages. The art of pairing herbs will be discussed in this section in order to maximize their medicinal benefits and address certain health issues. We can construct potent blends that help holistic healing and our general wellness by comprehending the complementary qualities of several plants.

Some herbs can be combined to treat common problems like indigestion, bloating, and gastrointestinal pain for people looking for digestive support. For example, ginger and peppermint are well known for their ability to aid in digestion. Ginger promotes digestion and lessens inflammation, while peppermint aids in calming the muscles of the digestive system. These two herbs paired produce a strong mixture that supports digestive equilibrium and calms the stomach.

A common health objective is to strengthen the immune system, particularly during times of seasonal change or when being exposed to pathogens. Elderberry and echinacea are two plants with a known benefits for enhancing the immune system. The immune system is boosted by echinacea, which also aids in the body's ability to fight off infections, and elderberry, which has antioxidant and antiviral qualities. A potent immune-boosting elixir is produced by pairing these herbs, supporting general immunological health.

Our wellbeing in today's fast-paced society depends on our ability to control our stress levels and find moments of tranquility. Herbs like chamomile and lavender are well known for their calming and unwinding qualities. While lavender offers calming characteristics that aid in stress relief and the promotion of tranquillity, chamomile encourages relaxation, lowers anxiety, and aids in sleep. These two herbs combined in a tea blend produce a calming elixir that soothes the body and mind.

Certain herbs can enhance overall lung function, calm irritated airways, and reduce congestion when it comes to respiratory health. Two herbs that are frequently utilized for respiratory health are eucalyptus and thyme. Thyme serves as an antibacterial and promotes respiratory health, while eucalyptus has expectorant characteristics that assist to loosen mucus and make breathing easier. When these herbs are combined, a strong infusion that supports comfortable breathing is produced.

Our physical health and emotional wellness are both crucial. Two herbs that are known for elevating mood are lemon balm and rosemary. While rosemary promotes memory and concentration, lemon balm provides relaxing effects, lowers stress, and enhances cognitive function. These herbs combined in a tea blend produce an uplifting elixir that promotes mental clarity, lowers stress levels, and uplifts mood.

Herbs having anti-inflammatory and analgesic effects can be used to create a relaxing blend for people looking for relief from joint and muscular pain. The anti-inflammatory benefits of ginger, turmeric, and devil's claw are well recognized, and devil's claw also has analgesic characteristics. These herbs combined in a tea blend produce a strong elixir that promotes joint and muscle health, lessens inflammation, and relieves pain.

We can utilize nature's healing abilities and create blends that cater to our particular wellness needs by pairing herbs for specific health benefits. We can create teas that support balance, vitality, and overall well-being by comprehending the characteristics of various herbs and their synergistic benefits.

It is essential to select high-quality herbs and utilize them in the right proportions when researching herb pairings for certain health advantages. To achieve the ideal balance of flavors and therapeutic effects, experiment with various ratios, mixtures, and steeping times. To guarantee compatibility with any existing medical problems or prescription drugs, think about consulting with a licensed herbalist or healthcare practitioner.

Accept the practice of pairing herbs for health benefits as a journey toward empowerment and self-care. Learn about the amazing potential of nature's medicine and enjoy the therapeutic benefits of herbal tea combinations created to meet your individual requirements. Each drink should serve as a reminder of the ability of herbs to support and nourish your body, mind, and soul.

Experimenting with spices and other additives

Herbal tea serves as a blank canvas for creative exploration in addition to being a delightful and soothing beverage. We may improve the flavors, aromas, and even health advantages of our herbal beverages by adding spices and other additives. In order to improve our herbal tea experience, we will explore the world of experimenting with spices and other additives in this section. This guide will motivate you to start a tasty adventure, regardless of whether your goals are to stimulate your senses, encourage certain health benefits, or simply enjoy new tastes.

The flavor profiles of herbal teas can be greatly improved by the use of spices. They can give the beverage depth, complexity, and a hint of warmth. For instance, cinnamon adds a wonderful sweetness and a hint of heat. Cloves add a warm, earthy tone, while cardamom adds a distinctive aroma. We can make a simple herbal infusion into an intriguing and complex beverage by experimenting with various spices.

Herbal teas can be enhanced with some spices known for their digestive benefits to help promote gastrointestinal health. For instance, ginger promotes digestion, lessens motion sickness, and eases gastrointestinal discomfort. Fennel seeds have carminative qualities that might ease indigestion and lessen bloating. When these spices are combined with herbs like chamomile or peppermint, a potent mixture that supports digestive health and alleviates typical digestive problems results.

Lemon, lime, and orange are examples of citrus fruits that can give herbal teas a colorful and energizing flavor. Their fragrant and zesty flavors stimulate the palette and arouse the senses. Citrus fruits are full of antioxidants and vitamin C, both of which support a healthy immune system. You can improve the flavor and nutritional value of your herbal brew by adding a squeeze of lemon juice or an orange slice.

To give herbal teas a hint of sweetness and depth, use herbal syrups and organic sweeteners. For instance, honey not only sweetens the beverage but also has anti-inflammatory and antibacterial qualities. While agave syrup offers a mild and low-glycemic substitute, maple syrup adds a deep and earthy flavor. Further enhancing the health advantages of the tea are herbal syrups prepared from ingredients like elderberry or rosehip that impart distinct flavors.

Roots with therapeutic benefits and adaptogenic qualities include licorice, ginseng, and astragalus. While ginseng and astragalus support vitality, resilience, and general wellbeing, licorice root adds a natural sweetness and eases the throat. These therapeutic roots can be steeped with herbs to make herbal tea blends that encourage balance and stress reduction.

Aromatic flowers and herbs can be added to create a sensory experience that is uplifting and calming. Lavender has a soft floral aroma and relaxing and stress-relieving effects. Rose petals give an air of romance and tranquility. Flowers with jasmine scents have a relaxing and aromatic effect. We can create herbal teas that appeal to our senses of taste and scent as well as our sensation of calm and wellbeing by experimenting with floral infusions.

Herbal teas can be flavored with herbal tinctures and extracts, which are concentrated versions of medicinal plants. They provide an easy method to add particular therapeutic characteristics to your brew. For instance, valerian extract encourages relaxation and sleep while echinacea tincture helps strengthen the immune system. Your herbal tea's medicinal properties can be improved by adding a few drops of these strong extracts, which can also offer targeted support for a range of health issues.

Explore exotic spices and ingredients from around the world to embark on a culinary journey. As an illustration, turmeric imparts a vibrant golden hue and has anti-inflammatory qualities. Green tea powdered matcha has a distinctive earthy flavor and gives you a slight energy boost. When added to herbal mixtures, star anise imparts a characteristic licorice-like flavor. We may broaden our palates and develop fascinating new combinations of herbs, spices, and additives by embracing world flavors.

A pleasant approach to discover new flavors, aromas, and health advantages in herbal tea is to experiment with different spices and other additives. We may improve the experience of drinking herbal tea and customize it to meet our own preferences and needs by adding spices, citrus fruits, herbal syrups, medicinal roots, floral infusions, and other innovative ingredients. Remember to start with little amounts, pay attention to your preferences and their impact on your body, and progressively hone your blends to perfection as you set out on your voyage of flavor exploration. Take pleasure in brewing customized, unique herbal tea blends that are good for the body and the soul.

Chapter V

Herbal Tea for
Health and Wellness

Overview of herbal teas for specific health conditions

Herbal teas have been used throughout history as natural remedies to treat a variety of ailments and to improve overall health and well-being. Each herb has distinct qualities and active ingredients that can address particular medical issues. We will explore the therapeutic advantages of herbal teas for various medical ailments in this section. Herbal teas provide a gentle and holistic approach to assist our entire wellness, from easing digestive difficulties to boosting immunity and fostering relaxation.

Digestive problems, like bloating, indigestion, and stomach discomfort, are frequent worries that can seriously lower our quality of life. Fortunately, a number of herbs are well known for their capacity to promote digestive health. With its calming and antispasmodic qualities, peppermint tea helps ease digestive discomfort and support a healthy digestive system. The anti-inflammatory and carminative effects of chamomile tea help to calm an upset stomach and lessen bloating. With its strong anti-nausea and digestive stimulating properties, ginger tea helps ease digestive discomfort.

A strong immune system is necessary for protecting the body from infections and preserving good health. Teas made from herbs can be quite helpful in promoting immunological health. Echinacea tea is well known for strengthening the immune system, assisting the body in warding off infections, and minimizing the intensity and length of cold and flu symptoms. Elderberry tea has antiviral and immune-boosting qualities and is high in antioxidants and flavonoids. When the immune system needs an extra boost or during cold and flu season, both teas are great choices.

Stress and anxiety are common problems that impact many people in today's fast-paced environment. Teas made from herbs can be a soothing and all-natural way to encourage relaxation and mental health. With its light sedative effects, chamomile tea can help lower anxiety and improve the quality of sleep. Tea made from lemon balm has a relaxing effect that helps with stress management and relaxation. With its calming scent and ability to reduce anxiety, lavender tea is popular. Incorporating these herbal teas in your daily routine can support the development of a calm and quiet mindset.

With the use of some herbal teas, respiratory ailments like coughing, congestion, and allergies can be relieved. As a natural decongestant, peppermint tea relieves nasal congestion and calms irritated airways. With its expectorant qualities, eucalyptus tea aids in mucus clearance and promotes respiratory health. The anti-inflammatory properties of nettle tea can reduce allergy and respiratory inflammation symptoms. These herbal teas provide a calming and organic way to support respiratory comfort.

For a person to remain in optimal health, the body's natural detoxification mechanisms must be supported. Herbal teas can enhance liver function and help the body remove toxins. Due to its diuretic characteristics, dandelion tea aids in detoxifying by raising urine production. Milk thistle tea promotes liver function and aids in the body's detoxification process. Tea made from burdock root aids in the elimination of toxins and waste by acting as a gentle blood cleanser. These teas can be used as a part of a healthy lifestyle or as part of a detoxification regimen.

For overall wellbeing, maintaining cardiovascular health is essential. By encouraging normal blood pressure, lowering cholesterol levels, and boosting circulation, herbal teas can benefit heart health. Due to its inherent ACE-inhibiting qualities, hibiscus tea can assist in lowering blood pressure. Hawthorn tea supports healthy cholesterol levels, strengthens the heart muscle, and enhances circulation. Green tea's abundance in antioxidants helps the heart by lowering inflammation and oxidative stress. These herbal teas can be a beneficial supplement to a heart-healthy lifestyle when used regularly.

Teas made from herbs can help with a variety of women's health issues, from monthly pain to menopausal symptoms. Mineral and vitamin-rich raspberry leaf tea is well known for toning the uterus and easing menstruation pains. As a result of the phytoestrogens included in red clover tea, hot flashes and other menopausal symptoms such as irritability may be lessened. Menstrual cycles can be regulated and menstrual discomfort can be reduced with the help of the popular herb dong quai tea in traditional Chinese medicine. For women looking for natural remedies to treat specific medical conditions, these herbal teas are available.

Teas made from herbs provide a wide range of medicinal advantages for many medical ailments. There is a herbal tea to meet your needs, whether you're looking for relief from digestive problems, immune system support, stress reduction, respiratory health, detoxification, heart health, or women's health concerns. The gentle and holistic approach of including these teas into your daily routine can help to promote general wellness. However, it's crucial to consult with a doctor before utilizing herbal teas for any particular health issues, especially if you have underlying illnesses or are taking medication.

Unlock the potential of herbal teas to improve your health and well-being by harnessing the power of nature.

Recipes for teas targeting digestion, sleep, stress relief, etc.

Herbal teas have long been valued for their curative qualities and capacity to calm the body as well as the mind. We can make enticing and therapeutic tea blends that precisely address common health problems using the wide variety of herbs that are readily available. In this section, we'll look at a variety of herbal tea recipes that can help with digestion, better sleep, stress relief, boosting the immune system, detoxification, and more. With the help of these recipes, you'll be able to take advantage of the herbal remedies that come naturally, creating enticing and potent teas that promote your overall well- being.

Our regular life might be disrupted by digestive problems, which can also affect our overall well-being. Fortunately, many plants have characteristics that promote a healthy digestive system. These herbs can be used in carefully formulated mixes to produce teas that reduce gastrointestinal discomfort and support ideal gut health. The Soothing Mint Blend is one such mixture. This blend of chamomile flowers, fennel seeds, and dried peppermint leaves provides a soothing yet potent treatment for stomach issues. Long renowned for its calming effects are peppermint, chamomile, and fennel seeds, which can help with digestion and lessen bloating.

We need a good night's sleep to maintain our general health and mental clarity. Herbal teas can assist to relax the body, soothe the mind, and encourage sound sleep. The appropriate combination of herbs can produce a calming elixir that improves the quality of sleep. The Tranquil Lavender Blend, which contains dried lavender flowers, lemon balm leaves, and chamomile flowers, is one recipe to take into consideration. While chamomile and lemon balm promote calmness and sound sleep, lavender is well known for its calming aroma and sleep-inducing effects.

Stress has become increasingly common in our fast-paced modern environment. Teas made from herbs can reduce stress and help you feel balanced and relaxed. We can make teas that reduce stress and bring harmony to the mind and body by choosing the proper herbs and combining them in strategic mixes. The Calming Chamomile Delight is a well-liked option for reducing stress. Dried lavender flowers, lemon verbena leaves, and chamomile flowers are included in this mixture. The calming effects of chamomile are well known, and lemon verbena and lavender also promote relaxation and relieve stress.

A healthy immune system is essential for overall well-being. Teas made from herbs that strengthen the immune system might be a beneficial addition to your wellness regimen. We can make teas that assist our body's natural defense mechanisms by adding selected herbs renowned for their immune-stimulating effects. Invigorating Elderberry Blend is an excellent recipe for immune system support. Elderberries, rose hips, and echinacea leaves are all dried in this mixture. Rose hips and echinacea also contribute to the immune system's strength while elderberries are an abundant source of immune-supporting antioxidants.

Body detoxification aids in toxin removal and equilibrium restoration. Detoxifying herbal teas can aid in this procedure and advance general health. We can make teas that help detoxification and our bodies natural cleansing processes by choosing herbs recognized for their purifying and cleansing properties. The Cleansing Green Tea Blend is a preferred option for detoxification. Dandelion root, nettle leaves, and dried green tea leaves are included in this mixture. Dandelion root and nettle strengthen and cleanse the liver, while green tea is high in antioxidants and well-known for its detoxification abilities.

Teas made from herbs are an excellent way to address certain health issues and enhance general wellbeing. By mastering the art of herbal tea blending, we can produce delicious blends that aid in detoxification, promote digestion, improve sleep quality, reduce stress, and more. We can unleash the amazing therapeutic potential of herbal teas by harnessing the power of nature and experimenting with different herbs and blends. A healthcare practitioner should always be consulted before introducing herbal teas into your diet, especially if you have underlying medical conditions or are taking medications, as individual responses to herbs might vary. Embrace the adventure of learning about the medicinal properties of herbs and raise your wellness through the skill of blending herbal teas. Cheers to a better, more energetic you!

Understanding the potential side effects and precautions

Due to its numerous health advantages and inherent healing abilities, herbal tea has experienced tremendous growth in popularity in recent years. It is important to understand that herbal teas might have negative effects and should be taken with caution, just like any medication. Despite being generally safe, herbs contain bioactive compounds that, if misused, might interact with medications, trigger allergic reactions, or have negative effects. In this section, we'll examine the possible negative effects of herbal teas, go through safety measures to take, and offer advice on how to drink herbal teas on a daily basis without getting sick.

Here are some of the possible adverse effects of herbal teas and the significance of comprehending and minimizing these risks. People can make educated decisions and guarantee the safe intake of herbal teas by being aware of allergic responses, interactions with medications, issues during pregnancy and nursing, and the potential for gastrointestinal discomfort.

Allergies are one of the possible negative effects of herbal teas. Herbs may cause allergic reactions in some people if they are exposed to them, and this reaction can occur after ingesting the herb. Skin rashes, itching, swelling, or respiratory symptoms like wheezing or breathing difficulties can all be signs of an allergic reaction. After ingesting herbal tea, it's crucial to watch out for any indications of allergic reactions. It is vital to stop consuming the herb and get medical help right once if any symptoms appear.

Herbal teas and medications can interact, which can either increase or decrease a drug's effects. It is crucial to understand that herbs include bioactive compounds that can impact a drug's metabolism and effectiveness. As an illustration, the herb St. John's Wort, which is frequently used to enhance mood, can interact with antidepressants and lessen their effectiveness. Before introducing herbal teas into their routine, people using medications should consult with a healthcare provider or pharmacist to establish their safety. This consultation will aid in identifying potential interactions and guard against any compromises in the security or efficacy of the medication.

Women who are pregnant or nursing should use caution when drinking herbal teas. During these times, certain medicines may have negative effects on uterine contractions or hormone levels. To find out which herbs are safe to ingest, pregnant and nursing women should seek advice from a healthcare provider. Based on the patient's health situation and any potential effects of herbs on pregnancy or nursing, healthcare providers can make particular recommendations.

Some herbs, especially those having laxative effects like senna or cascara sagrada, can upset the stomach when ingested in large doses or over an extended length of time. These herbs are frequently used for their inherent cleansing characteristics, but prolonged or excessive use might result in symptoms like diarrhea, cramps in the stomach, or discomfort. It is best to use these herbs cautiously and under a doctor's supervision, especially for the purposes for which they are meant.

It is crucial to prioritize safety and make informed judgments when introducing herbal teas into your daily routine. The following discussion covers the precautions and recommendations for the safe consumption of herbal teas, highlighting the significance of learning and education, quality and sourcing, starting cautiously, getting professional assistance, and encouraging variation and rotation. People can benefit from herbal teas while reducing risks and ensuring a safe and pleasurable tea-drinking experience by adhering to these recommendations.

It is essential to carry out in-depth study and familiarize yourself with the particular herbs you intend to employ before incorporating herbal teas into your routine. You can choose the herbs that are appropriate for your specific situation by being aware of their qualities, potential side effects, and contraindications. Reliable sources, like reputable books, peer-reviewed journals, or dependable websites, can offer useful information to help you make decisions and ensure safe consumption.

Herb quality is crucial to ensure its safety and effectiveness. It is crucial to purchase herbs from dependable and reputable sources. Look for suppliers who have earned a reputation for quality, sustainability, and openness in their farming and production methods or who have earned an organic certification. Ingesting herbs that might be contaminated with pesticides, heavy metals, or other harmful substances is less likely as a result. You can improve the safety and potency of your herbal tea preparations by selecting high-quality herbs.

It is best to start with small doses when introducing a new herbal tea into your regimen and gradually raise the dosage if well-tolerated. By using this method, you can monitor how your body reacts to the herb and look for any possible side effects. Starting out gradually also allows your body time to get used to the new herb and lessens the possibility of discomfort or unfavorable reactions. You can guarantee a seamless transition and reap the rewards of herbal teas without overdosing your body by being cautious.

Before introducing herbal teas into your regimen, it is essential to get advice from a healthcare provider or certified herbalist if you have underlying medical concerns, are taking medication, are pregnant, or are nursing a baby. These experts can offer individualized guidance, taking into account your unique medical requirements and any potential drug interactions. They can assist in determining which herbs are secure and suitable for your circumstance, ensuring that you get the most out of herbal teas while lowering any possible hazards.

It is advised to include a range of herbal teas in your regimen and switch up your tea selections to maintain balance and reduce the danger of developing sensitivities or accumulating excessive levels of particular ingredients. By varying your intake of herbs, you can guarantee a larger spectrum of bioactive compounds and therapeutic characteristics. Each plant has a unique set of advantages. A balanced and sustainable approach to drinking herbal tea is promoted by routinely rotating herbs, which decreases the possibility of overexposure to any one herb or its components.

The promotion of health and wellbeing using herbal teas is all-natural and holistic. But it's crucial to be aware of any possible adverse effects and safety measures related to their ingestion. People can make educated judgments and put their health first by being aware of potential allergic responses, drug interactions, and special measures for certain populations, such as pregnant women. People can safely take advantage of the health advantages of herbal teas by doing careful study, finding high-quality herbs, starting lightly, getting professional assistance when necessary, and exercising variation and rotation. To maximize the benefits of herbal teas for a healthier and more balanced life, keep in mind that responsible use and mindful consumption are essential.

Consulting with a healthcare professional when necessary

Herbal tea has long been valued for its healing abilities and all-encompassing approach to wellness. As people look for herbal tea advantages and natural remedies, it's important to recognize the importance of consulting healthcare experts. Although herbal teas are usually regarded as harmless, they include bioactive compounds which can interact with medications, have an influence on particular health conditions, or necessitate personalized guidance for specific individuals. This section discusses the value of seeking advice from medical professionals when thinking about drinking herbal tea, emphasizing their experience in assuring a safe and successful integration of herbal teas into one's wellness path.

Healthcare professionals are necessary in assuring safety, efficacy, and individualized advice when it comes to adding herbal teas into our wellness routines. Personalized health assessments, taking into account individual health goals, the significance of ongoing monitoring and evaluation, and the significance of healthcare professionals in the context of herbal tea consumption are all discussed below. Individuals can confidently navigate the complexity of herbal teas and improve their health and well-being by closely collaborating with healthcare specialists.

The understanding of medications, including their modes of action and potential interactions with herbal components, is significant among healthcare practitioners. This knowledge is essential for evaluating a person's pharmaceutical regimen and identifying possible interactions or contraindications. Understanding how specific herbs may interfere with prescription efficacy or produce side effects is crucial for people with chronic health issues who depend on prescribed pharmaceuticals to manage their wellbeing. To guarantee the secure incorporation of herbs into current treatment plans, healthcare professionals can offer advice and suggest suitable herbal teas.

Conducting complete health evaluations that take into account a person's particular circumstances is one of the main responsibilities of healthcare providers. The suitability of particular herbs might be considerably impacted by elements like underlying medical disorders, allergies, pregnancy, nursing, or age. Healthcare professionals can discover any contraindications or precautions through a thorough review, ensuring that people make educated decisions about the herbs they wish to include in their wellness regimens. Healthcare specialists can make customized suggestions and guarantee the secure integration of herbal teas on the basis of personalized health assessments.

When advising on the use of herbal tea, healthcare professionals take into account the specific health goals of the patient. Healthcare experts take these objectives into account when discussing herbal teas, regardless of whether the purpose is to treat particular symptoms, control chronic diseases, or improve overall well-being. They have the knowledge to suggest herbs that support a person's health objectives while also taking into account how well the herbs work with other therapies and lifestyle choices. Healthcare specialists make sure that herbal teas fit into a person's entire wellness strategy by factoring in their health objectives.

The impact of herbal teas on a person's health can be continuously monitored and assessed with the help of regular visits to medical professionals. In order to determine whether the selected herbal teas are having the desired effects, healthcare experts have the expertise and experience necessary. They can address any new issues, offer advice on possible herbal regimen modifications, and track general health improvement. This all-encompassing wellness strategy makes sure that people get continual care, empowering them to choose how much herbal tea to drink. Herbal teas are best incorporated into a person's lifestyle with regular monitoring and evaluation.

When we incorporate herbal teas into our everyday routines, consulting with healthcare specialists has several advantages. The integration of herbal teas with conventional treatment, their role in ensuring safety and efficacy, and their capacity to make tailored suggestions are all a result of their extensive knowledge and experience in herbal medicine. The benefits of consulting with medical experts, emphasizing their familiarity with herbal remedies, and the positive role they play in maximizing the health advantages of drinking herbal tea are highlighted below.

Healthcare professionals can confidently handle the complexity of herbal teas since they have in-depth understanding of herbal medicine. They are quite knowledgeable about the medicinal benefits, recommended dosages, and possible negative effects of certain herbs. Their knowledge makes sure that people have access to reliable, factual information so they can decide on the herbs they will take. People can benefit from the wealth of knowledge that healthcare professionals possess and obtain a deeper understanding of the herbs by consulting with them. This will enable them to optimize the health advantages of drinking herbal tea.

One of the key benefits of talking with medical experts is their capacity to offer a holistic viewpoint that takes into account the fusion of herbal teas with traditional medical therapies. The potential interactions between herbal teas and prescribed medications are well-known to healthcare practitioners. This information guarantees that treatment outcomes are neither compromised or subject to conflicts. Individuals can easily incorporate herbal teas into their overall wellness plan by collaborating with healthcare providers, encouraging a unified approach to health and wellbeing.

The effectiveness and safety of herbal teas are closely monitored by healthcare professionals. They can monitor a person's response to the herbs, analyze any potential adverse effects, and change the herbal regimen as needed through routine check-ins. This proactive strategy guarantees that people can benefit from herbal teas while reducing any possible risks. Healthcare professionals act as a compass, offering constant support and direction to make sure that drinking herbal tea is always safe and beneficial.

Healthcare experts recognize the value of making personalized suggestions based on a patient's unique health profile because every person is unique. When giving recommendations, they take into account things like current medical conditions, allergies, medications, and individual health objectives. Healthcare practitioners adopt a specialized strategy when choosing herbs to treat particular symptoms, figuring out the right dosage, or spotting potential problems. Healthcare specialists can help people choose the herbs that are best suited to their needs by taking into account their unique situations, maximizing the advantages of drinking herbal tea.

It's important to navigate the consultation procedure with a licensed healthcare practitioner while looking for advice on drinking herbal tea. Following are the stages to successfully navigating the consultation process, including selecting the best healthcare practitioner, getting ready for the consultation, keeping lines of communication open, and adhering to suggestions to track progress. By adhering to these recommendations, people can get the most out of their session and obtain tailored guidance that fits their requirements and objectives in terms of health.

Choosing a herbal medicine specialist who is a competent healthcare expert is the first step in the consultation procedure. This could include naturopaths, herbalists, or integrative medicine experts as well as general practitioners who are familiar with herbal medicines. It is crucial to select a specialist who is knowledgeable in herbal medicine, has relevant experience, and is aware of your unique medical requirements. Making sure you are working with a reputable professional can be achieved by investigating their credentials, area of specialization, and prior experience.

It's crucial to be prepared for your consultation in order to get the most out of it. Obtain pertinent details about your medical background, such as any current illnesses, allergies, and previous treatments. Make a list of all prescription and over-the-counter medications you are taking, as well as any dietary supplements, as they can interact with herbal teas. Take into account your health objectives as well as any particular concerns or queries you might have regarding drinking herbal tea. By having this information on hand, you give the healthcare provider a thorough picture of your health profile, enabling them to offer recommendations that are more well-informed.

Fostering honest and open communication with the healthcare provider is essential during the consultation. Share your health objectives, herbal tea preferences, and any concerns or adverse effects you may have encountered. By working together, the healthcare provider can develop a comprehensive understanding of your needs and then customize their recommendations. Additionally, it fosters a supportive and trusting relationship, which enables you to get the most relevant and specialized advice.

Following the appointment, it is crucial to follow the advice given by the healthcare provider and carefully track your progress. Pay attention to their recommendations for dose, frequency, and herb choice. Pay close attention to any changes in your symptoms, any adverse effects, or any possible drug interactions. Tracking advancement over time can be made easier by keeping a journal or making observations. For continuous help and direction, communicate any concerns or questions right away to the healthcare provider. You can plan routine follow-up sessions to assess your development and make any required modifications to your herbal tea diet.

Promoting the safe and efficient use of these natural medicines requires consulting with medical professionals regarding the use of herbal tea. When it comes to maximizing the advantages of herbal teas while lowering risks, their knowledge of herb-drug interactions, individualized health assessments, consideration of individual health goals, and continual monitoring and evaluation are crucial. Individuals can securely incorporate herbal teas into their wellness routines and ensure a comprehensive approach to health and well-being by working with healthcare specialists. Accepting the advice of medical specialists enables people to make knowledgeable decisions and explore the world of herbal teas with assurance.

<h1 style="text-align:center">Chapter VI</h1>

<h1 style="text-align:center">Herbal Tea Beyond Drinking</h1>

Alternative uses for herbal teas (e.g., in cooking, beauty routines)

Teas made from herbs have long been cherished for their healing qualities and mouthwatering flavors. Although they are typically used as calming beverages, their versatility goes beyond the teacup. This section explores the additional applications for herbal teas, including how they might improve recipes and be incorporated into cosmetic regimens. Herbal teas provide a natural and holistic approach to wellbeing that goes beyond the domain of customary tea drinking, from deepening recipes to nourishing the skin and hair.

Herbal teas provide culinary creations distinctive flavors and fragrances. Depending on the herbs used, infusing food with herbal tea can add subtle or prominent flavors. For instance, peppermint tea gives savory dishes a refreshing zing, while chamomile tea gives desserts a delicate floral touch. The flavor profile of numerous recipes can be improved by chefs and home cooks by using herbal tea in place of water or stock.

Teas made from herbs can be used to flavor meat, poultry, and vegetables. The taste and tenderness of the foods are improved as a result of the natural herbs and botanicals infusing them with their essence. Similar to this, adding herbal tea infusions to oils, vinegar, or syrups gives dressings, sauces, and sweet dishes a pleasant touch. There are endless choices, such as rosemary-infused honey or lavender-infused olive oil.

Desserts and baked items can benefit from the aromatic and therapeutic qualities of herbal teas. Bakers can make intriguing desserts by integrating tea infusions into batters, creams, and fillings. Matcha tea gives pastries a vivid green tint and a tinge of bitterness, while Earl Grey tea can turn a plain vanilla cake into a fragrant pleasure. The only restriction is one's creativity; the options are limitless.

Herbal teas are wonderful additions to beauty regimens since they have many skin-friendly properties. Calendula tea is excellent for reducing skin irritations and fostering a healthy complexion because it has calming and anti-inflammatory effects. Antioxidants included in green tea can help prevent the appearance of wrinkles and environmental damage to the skin. The skin can be revitalized and nourished by using cooled herbal tea compresses topically or by using face masks and toners with tea infusions.

Teas made from herbs can improve the condition and appearance of hair. For instance, rosemary tea is well recognized for its energizing qualities, which encourage hair growth and enhance scalp health. While nettle tea can help treat dandruff and maintain a healthy scalp, chamomile tea can naturally lighten hair and add shine. Natural remedies for various hair issues can be found by incorporating herbal tea rinses or tea-infused hair products into a hair care routine.

Teas made from herbs have long been connected to self-care practices and relaxation. Herbal tea may add a calming and pleasant sensation to the bathwater, which can aid in mind and body relaxation. For instance, peppermint tea can energize and refresh, while lavender tea can encourage peacefulness and help with stress reduction. The self-care experience is further improved by adding herbal tea to face steams or utilizing tea-infused sachets as aromatherapy tools.

Herbal teas can be used for a variety of purposes aside from their traditional use as soothing drinks. People can access a world of flavors and wellness advantages by using herbal teas into their beauty and cooking regimens. Herbal teas provide a natural and holistic approach to culinary innovation and self-care, from improving the flavor of dishes and infusing distinctive smells to nourishing the skin and hair. Embracing the flexibility of herbal teas provides us countless opportunities to explore and utilize nature's power in several spheres of our existence. Therefore, the next time you go for a cup of herbal tea, take into account the plethora of alternative applications that might improve your culinary explorations and beauty rituals.

Recipes for incorporating herbal teas into food and desserts

For their therapeutic qualities and fragrant characteristics, herbal teas have long been valued. While enjoying a warm cup of herbal tea on its own is a delight, these adaptable infusions may also be utilized to add richness and depth to a variety of culinary preparations. The skill of mixing herbal teas into cuisine and desserts will be discussed in this section. By doing so, we can discover a world of flavors and give conventional recipes a unique twist.

Herbal teas can add taste and health benefits to soups and broths by infusing them with their distinctive smells. A vegetable soup with chamomile tea as the foundation, for instance, has a delicate floral note that balances the earthy flavors of the vegetables. Similar to this, Asian-inspired soups benefit from a lemongrass and ginger tea-infused broth that gives them a zesty and energizing flavor.

Natural tenderization and flavor infusion can be achieved by marinating meats and shellfish in herbal tea infusions. For instance, a marinade made of green tea and citrus offers a light, slightly bitter flavor to grilled chicken, while a marinade made of lavender gives roasted salmon a delicate floral flavor. The herbal tea infusions work their culinary wonders to produce dishes that are flavorful and luscious.

The flavor of salads, roasted vegetables, or pasta dishes can be enhanced by using herbal teas as the base for delectable dressings and sauces. For a flavorful and savory dressing, think about combining honey, balsamic vinegar, and rosemary tea-infused olive oil. As an alternative, roasted veggies can be topped with a tart lemon and mint tea reduction for a burst of freshness.

Herbal teas can be made into delicious dessert sauces that give sweet concoctions more depth and character. For instance, a simple scoop of vanilla ice cream can be transformed into a gourmet treat by adding a cinnamon and chai tea-infused caramel sauce. Lemon pound cake pairs nicely with a lavender and honey syrup, which may also be drizzled over fresh berries to create a sophisticated and fragrant dessert.

Herbal teas add distinctive flavors and fragrances to baked goods when they are incorporated into them. Imagine a rich, buttery pound cake that has been infused with a fragrant Earl Grey tea flavor. Matcha tea may give cookies and cakes a vivid green hue and a little bitter undertone, resulting in aesthetically pleasing and tasty desserts.

Herbal tea infusions can be added to frostings and creams to enhance them and make them delectable toppings for cakes, pastries, or even fruit platters. A fresh fruit tart goes perfectly with chamomile tea-infused whipped cream, while a traditional chocolate cake is elevated to new levels of indulgence with peppermint tea-infused cream cheese frosting.

Herbal teas can be used to infuse different ingredients to produce distinctive flavors and sensations. For custards, ice creams, or panna cotta, for instance, infusing milk or cream with lavender tea yields a subtle floral base. Cocktails or mocktails get a bright color and acidic flavor boost from hibiscus tea-infused syrups, which also give your drinks a light, fruity flavor.

Herbal teas can give conventional jams and preserves a unique twist. For instance, a breakfast spread with berry and rosehip tea-infused jam has a light acidity and floral notes. Toast or scones are given a delightful twist by a marmalade made with citrusy bergamot and orange tea.

Although herbal teas are frequently consumed as independent drinks, they can also serve as the base for a variety of energizing mocktails and other drinks. For example, a lively and alcohol-free drink alternative for parties or special events can be made by combining a fruity and aromatic herbal tea, such as berry or citrus blends, with sparkling water, fresh fruit, and herbs.

A fun and inventive approach to experience the numerous flavors and aromatic qualities that herbal teas has to offer is to incorporate them into meals and desserts. The options range from savory dishes to sweet delights. Our favorite recipes can be given extra dimension, character, and a hint of natural goodness by using herbal teas into a variety of culinary creations. So, use herbal teas as your secret ingredient and let your creativity run wild as you set off on a culinary adventure. Cheers to the delicious combinations of flavors and pleasant surprises found in each bite and sip!

DIY herbal tea-infused skincare and haircare products

Herbal teas have emerged as potent companions in our pursuit of healthy skin and hair, and the beauty industry has seen a considerable movement toward natural ingredients. We may develop individualized, efficient, and greener alternatives to commercial products by utilizing the inherent qualities of herbs and incorporating them into skincare and haircare products. The potential of botanicals for glowing skin and luscious locks will be unlocked as we explore the world of DIY herbal tea-infused skincare and haircare products.

Herbal teas have several advantages for the skin and can be used as the base for a variety of skincare products. Their capacity to efficiently and gently wash and tone the skin is one of their main advantages. For instance, a chamomile tea infusion can relax and soothe inflamed or sensitive skin, while a toner made from green tea can provide antioxidant benefits and help reduce inflammation. These organic treatments can be used topically with cotton pads or as ingredients in homemade cleaning solutions.

Another well-liked approach to incorporate herbal teas into beauty regimens is through facial masks and steams. These procedures help nurture and renew the skin. For instance, a calendula and chamomile tea steam can open pores and support a healthy complexion, while a lavender and rose petal tea mask can offer a calming and moisturizing treatment. These at-home spa experiences are provided by these DIY procedures.

Additionally, face serums and moisturizers with herbal tea infusions can provide the skin a potent boost of nutrients and antioxidants. While a combination of hibiscus tea and rosehip oil can offer anti-aging benefits and increase skin suppleness, an aloe vera gel and green tea infusion can be combined to make a light and moisturizing serum. These organic mixtures can be altered to handle particular skin issues and offer a tailored skincare procedure.

Teas made from herbs can also do wonders for our hair, nourishing it and enhancing its general health. Herbal tea-infused hair rinses and sprays might improve the gloss and vigor of our hair. For instance, a chamomile tea spray can add luster and highlights to blonde or light-colored hair, while a rosemary tea rinse can promote hair development and enhance scalp health. These easy home remedies can be applied as leave-in treatments or after shampooing.

Our handmade shampoos and conditioners can be customized to meet our individual needs by using herbal teas. For instance, a shampoo infused with nettle and green tea can fight dandruff and encourage the growth of healthy hair, and a conditioner infused with hibiscus tea can hydrate and strengthen hair strands. By offering a natural substitute to commercial treatments loaded with harsh chemicals, these compositions make sure that our hair gets the attention it needs.

Herbal tea-infused scalp treatments and hair masks help stimulate the scalp and hydrate the hair follicles. An herbal tea-infused scalp treatment with peppermint and tea tree oil, for instance, can ease itching and encourage blood flow. A deep conditioning hair mask made of henna and chamomile tea can bring out natural highlights. With the ability to be customized, these treatments provide a natural and individualized approach to haircare.

There are a few crucial suggestions to bear in mind while formulating skincare and haircare products infused with herbal tea. First and foremost, it's important to choose the right herbs based on your individual requirements and concerns. To produce formulas that are specifically customized to your desired results, research the qualities of various herbs and their advantages for the skin and hair.

Second, the effectiveness of the finished goods depends greatly on the quality of the herbs. To make sure you are utilizing all of the medicinal compounds in your herbs, choose organic, high-quality herbs. Herbs' purity and freshness can be ensured by growing them yourself or purchasing from reliable vendors.

Furthermore, for good herbal tea infusions, understanding the proper extraction techniques is essential. Different methods, such as steeping, simmering, or cold-infusion, might be used depending on the qualities of the herbs. Knowing how to extract each herb properly makes sure that the necessary qualities are successfully included into the skincare or haircare product.

Finally, to maintain their efficacy, homemade herbal tea-infused products should be stored properly. To protect the formulations from light and maintain their efficacy, store them in dark glass containers and keep them in a cool, dry environment. Additionally, it is crucial to keep track of each product's shelf life and eliminate those that are beginning to spoil or have passed their expiration date.

A natural and holistic approach to beauty is provided through homemade herbal tea-infused skincare and haircare products. We can take care of our skin and hair while avoiding the use of harsh chemicals if we incorporate the healing power of herbs into our everyday routines. The possibilities are limitless, from calming chamomile toners to energizing rosemary hair rinses to nourishing hibiscus face serums. Discover the secrets of nature for glowing skin and lush hair by embracing the charm of herbal teas. Reconnect with the knowledge of the past and set off on a journey of self-care while utilizing the natural benefits of herbal teas. Let the natural beauty of botanicals turn your hair- and skin-care routines into indulgent and relaxing experiences.

Creative ideas for gifting herbal tea blends

Finding moments of peace and relaxation has become more crucial in a society when daily life is busy and hectic. Herbal tea blends are the ideal solution when looking for thoughtful and unique gifts for our loved ones. These carefully and thoughtfully made blends offer an appealing diversion from the pressures of daily life. In this section, we'll look at unique gifting suggestions for herbal tea blends so that we can spread the love of herbal infusions and encourage wellness through the art of giving.

Giving customized blends based on recipient tastes and needs is one of the great features of herbal tea blends. We can add care and compassion to our presents by hand-crafting distinctive blends, making them really unique.

Start by choosing a range of premium herbs and botanicals that offer a diversity of tastes, fragrances, and potential health advantages. Use chamomile, lavender, and lemon balm to make a tranquil combination. Use mint, green tea, and citrus zest to make a reviving blend. Try out various ratios and combinations to produce flavor profiles that are harmonious and appealing to the recipient's palate.

When giving herbal tea blends as presents, packaging is crucial. Choose attractive tin or beautiful glass jars to exhibit the herbs' rich colors and textures while also preserving their freshness. The package can be given a unique touch by adding decorations like ribbons, labels, or personalized phrases to make it more eye-catching and memorable. Not only does it add value, but it also guarantees that the receiver will be able to enjoy their tea to the maximum by including brewing instructions and a list of ingredients.

The ability to create a unique and unified experience for the recipient is offered by themed gift packages. We can build a theme that resonates with the recipient and leaves a positive impression by taking into account their interests, preferences, or particular occasions.

Combine a relaxing herbal tea blend with luxurious bath products, scented candles, and a soft, snuggly robe to create a Relaxation Retreat gift set. This combination encourages rest and self-care while providing the receiver with a revitalizing break from the pressures of daily life.

Include a yoga mat, a journal for mindfulness exercises, a set of essential oils, and several herbal tea blends known for their health advantages in a gift box called Wellness and Balance. This gift package encourages the recipient to adopt a balanced lifestyle and fosters a holistic approach to well-being.

Consider a Nature's Harvest gift set to commemorate the splendor of nature throughout the seasons. Include herbal tea blends that highlight herbs that are in season, such as peppermint in the winter, elderflower in the spring, hibiscus in the summer, and cinnamon and ginger in the fall. With the help of this gift set, the recipient can experience the tastes and scents unique to each season, strengthening their connection to the year's natural cycles.

Include homemade tea accessories or additional items that go well with the herbal tea blends to make giving more enjoyable. These improvements show consideration and offer useful tea-drinking equipment.

Give handmade tea infusers as gifts, such as glass teapots with built-in infusers, metal mesh balls, or fabric sachets. Make these items distinctive and reflect the recipient's individuality by adding decorative charms or personalized tags.

A tea recipe booklet featuring handmade herbal tea recipes is yet another unique concept. Pair this booklet with the herbal tea blends to give the recipient ideas and pointers for experimenting with various tea concoctions and appreciating the art of blending on their own.

The tea experience can be enhanced further by complementary gifts. For instance, a jar of homemade infused honey or a selection of premium honey might bring a hint of natural sweetness to the tea. A set of exquisite tea cups or mugs with beautiful engravings or motifs can enhance the tea-drinking experience and serve as priceless memories.

The skill of giving herbal tea blends as gifts combines the beauty of nature, blending creativity, and the joy of giving. We can make presents that are genuinely meaningful and memorable by making personalized blends, creating themed gift sets, and integrating DIY additions and complementary items. Take advantage of the opportunity to delve into the huge world of herbs, try out new flavors, and create beautiful packaging. The beauty and nourishment of herbal infusions will inspire you to unleash your creativity and delight your loved ones. As you begin your giving adventure, keep in mind that the real gift isn't just the tea; it's also the peace, joy, and connection it offers to people who receive it. Spread warmth, wellness, and love one cup at a time by unwrapping the gift-giving wonder of herbal tea.

Chapter VII

Embracing Sustainability
and Ethical Practices

The importance of sourcing sustainable and organic herbs

It is essential to pause to reflect on the sources of the products we consume in the fast-paced world of today, where convenience frequently takes precedence. Purchasing organic and sustainably grown herbs is not only a moral decision, but it is also an investment in our health and the welfare of the earth. In this section, we will examine the value of obtaining organic and sustainably grown herbs and the advantages they provide for both people and the environment.

Sustainable herb sourcing involves methods that preserve the delicate balance between environmental protection and human consumption. It entails protecting the environments that enable herb development, fostering biodiversity, and guaranteeing long-term supply for future generations.

Herb cultivation using organic farming techniques is a critical component of sustainability. Synthetic pesticides, herbicides, and fertilizers that are hazardous to the environment and human health are not used in organic farming. Instead, it places an emphasis on using environmentally friendly methods to preserve soil fertility and ecological balance, such as crop rotation, composting, and biological pest control.

Another crucial aspect of sustainable sourcing is supporting regional and small-scale herb growers. By purchasing herbs from local producers, we support local economies, preserve traditional agricultural techniques, and lessen the carbon emissions brought on by long-distance shipping. Supporting small-scale farmers also guarantees that traditional knowledge and experience are passed down through the generations and contributes to maintaining the diversity of herb kinds.

Protecting wild herb populations is another aspect of sustainable sourcing. Overharvesting has the potential to deplete natural habitats and endanger the survival of some species. Respecting harvest restrictions, protecting natural habitats, and supporting programs that encourage the regeneration of wild herb populations are all part of ethical wild harvesting practices.

Choosing organic herbs goes beyond protecting the environment. By limiting our exposure to potentially harmful chemicals and encouraging the consumption of pure, unadulterated herbs, it is a commitment to prioritizing our general well-being and health.

Herbs that are grown conventionally frequently have residues of artificial pesticides and other agricultural chemicals, which when consumed can be harmful to your health. By selecting organic herbs, we reduce the possibility of consuming these dangerous compounds, shielding our families and ourselves from potential health risks.

Additionally, organic herbs are grown in nutrient-rich soils without the use of artificial fertilizers. As a result, herbs become more nutrient-dense and have higher concentrations of healthy compounds like vitamins, minerals, and antioxidants. The herbs' medicinal benefits are enhanced by the higher nutrient content, which encourages their healing effects and general wellbeing.

The herb production method is ensured to adhere to strict guidelines and standards due to organic certification. This includes keeping track of the inputs being used, preserving soil fertility, fostering biodiversity, and respecting moral standards. By assisting growers of organic herbs, we help organic farming continue to expand and encourage more farmers to use ecologically friendly growing methods.

The ecology is greatly impacted by purchasing herbs that are grown sustainably and organically. It lessens the detrimental consequences of conventional agricultural operations and protects ecosystems and natural resources.

Fertility and soil health are given priority in organic farming techniques. Organic herb production eliminates soil erosion, water pollution, and the use of synthetic fertilizers and chemicals. The demand for excessive irrigation is reduced and water resources are conserved when soils are healthy because they hold moisture more effectively. Additionally, using organic farming methods encourages the retention of carbon in the soil, reducing climate change and aiding in carbon sequestration.

Sustainable herb procurement aids in the preservation of biodiversity. Habitats for various plant and animal species are created by herb farms that put an emphasis on ecological balance. They support crop pollination by encouraging pollinators like bees and butterflies, which are essential for maintaining the health of the ecosystem. Maintaining biodiversity improves natural pest control, strengthens resilient ecosystems, and lessens the need for chemical interventions.

Additionally, sustainable herb sourcing lessens the environmental impact of producing and transporting herbs. By selecting locally grown herbs, we reduce the amount of greenhouse gases produced by long-distance transportation and help to create more regionalized, sustainable food systems.

Sustainable and organic herb sourcing is not just a trend; it's a deliberate decision with far-reaching effects on our health, the environment, and future generations. By employing sustainable methods for growing herbs, we promote biodiversity, protect the ecosystems' delicate balance, and help keep old-fashioned farming techniques alive. By lowering our exposure to dangerous chemicals and guaranteeing that we are consuming pure, nutrient-rich botanicals, choosing organic herbs protects our health.

It is crucial to support environmentally friendly herb producers, local organizations, and activities in a world where our choices affect the future. We become stewards of nature's abundance and nurture the delicate interconnection between people and the earth by embracing sustainable and organic herb procurement. Let's go on a journey of mindful consumerism, where each cup of herbal tea signifies a dedication to our health, the sustainability of future generations, and the health of the earth.

Tips for growing your own herbal garden

Humans and plants have a close relationship, and herbs have always been important in our lives, providing culinary delights, natural remedies, and sensory pleasures. You can harness the power of nature right outside your door by creating your own herbal garden, which is a fulfilling and empowering experience. In this section, we will explore the skill of maintaining a herbal garden and offer you helpful advice so that you can start on this enlightening journey.

The area you choose for your herbal garden will determine its success. Choose a location that receives at least six hours of direct sunlight each day because most plants like places with plenty of sunlight. Make sure the soil has good drainage to avoid waterlogging, which can cause root rot. Additionally, take into account the microclimate of your area and choose herbs that are appropriate for the local climatic circumstances and growing conditions.

Spend some time planning and designing your herbal garden before you begin planting. Take into account elements like the size of the garden, the herbs you wish to plant, and their particular needs. Herbs with similar requirements can be grouped together to make maintenance and care easier. You can design a mixed garden that provides a variety of herbs for various uses, or you can arrange your garden by theme (cuisine herbs, medicinal herbs, etc.).

Your herbal garden can be started in one of two ways: by starting with seeds or by buying seedlings from nurseries. You can observe a plant's whole lifecycle, from seed to harvest, by growing herbs from seeds. It does, however, demand more time and focus. On the other hand, seedlings provide a head start and are a practical choice for beginners or people with limited time. Regardless of the procedure, make sure the seeds or seedlings are of a high-quality and obtained from reputable sources.

Your herbal garden's health and growth depend on how well the soil has been prepared. Most herbs demand soil that is well-drained and rich with organic matter. Compost or other organic matter can be added to the soil to increase its fertility and structure. The planting location should be cleared of any grass or weeds, and the soil should be loosened to provide a favorable environment for root growth. Follow the planting instructions for each herb's recommended spacing to ensure adequate air circulation and growth.

Keeping a healthy herbal garden requires regular watering. Avoid overwatering as it might cause root damage because most herbs require appropriate moisture levels. When the top inch of the soil seems dry, check the soil's moisture content and water your herbs. Mulching around the plants can aid in moisture retention and slow the growth of weeds. Check your herbs frequently for pests and illnesses, and take the necessary precautions to protect them, such as using organic pest management techniques or companion planting.

The satisfaction of a herb garden comes from gathering and using the plants you have cultivated. Herbs should be harvested in the morning when the essential oils are most potent. Cut the herbs just above a group of sound leaves or nodes using razor-sharp scissors or pruning shears. Herbs should totally dry before being stored or used. Different herbs require different drying techniques, such as hanging bundles upside-down, dehydrating, or air-drying. To maintain their effectiveness, properly dried herbs can be kept in airtight containers in a cool, dark location.

Your herbal garden can expand as your passion for herbs does. By introducing new herbs or experimenting with various varieties, you might want to increase the size of your garden. To make sure your existing garden can support each herb, learn about its individual needs. To make the most of confined space and develop a varied and vibrant herbal oasis, you may also consider companion planting, container gardening, and vertical gardening.

A journey that fosters a connection with nature, gives you the power to take control of your health and wellbeing, and provides a bounty of aromatic, culinary, and therapeutic delights is cultivating your own herbal garden. By using the recommendations provided in this section, you can establish a flourishing herbal garden that not only enhances the appearance of your surroundings but also gives you a sustainable and endless supply of fresh herbs. Accept the magic of nature, take good care of your garden, and enjoy the plentiful pleasures that are waiting for you in your own herbal paradise.

Ethical considerations in herbal tea production

Due to their numerous therapeutic capabilities, pleasant aromas, and countless health advantages, herbal teas have become extremely popular. It is critical to look into the ethical issues related to the production of herbal teas as consumer demand for them increases. Sustainability, fair trade, worker rights, biodiversity preservation, and community empowerment are just a few examples of the many values that make up ethical behaviors. To maintain a sustainable and fair industry, we will examine the ethical issues involved in the manufacturing of herbal tea in this section. We will emphasize the value of making informed decisions.

Sustainable farming methods are the cornerstone of the production of ethical herbal tea. Sustainable farming aims to reduce environmental effect, maintain healthy soil, and save biodiversity. It uses methods including agroforestry, regenerative agriculture, organic farming, and permaculture. Farmers of herbal tea contribute to better ecosystems, reduce chemical residues in the teas, and protect the health of farmworkers and consumers by refraining from using synthetic pesticides, herbicides, and fertilizers.

An essential component of producing herbal tea ethically is biodiversity preservation. Many of the herbs used in teas come from wild populations or are grown in their natural habitats. To avoid overharvesting and guarantee the long-term survival of plant species, sustainable harvesting techniques should be used. The conservation of biodiversity and priceless genetic resources is enhanced through promoting seed saving and exchange programs, cultivating herbs in harmony with nature, and supporting projects to save endangered plant species.

The social and economic facets of the industry are taken into account when making herbal tea. Assuring fair wages and working conditions for farmers and workers, as well as empowering communities, are all goals of fair trade practices. The assurance that the tea was produced ethically is provided through fair trade certifications. Supporting fair trade herbal teas contributes to the improvement of farming communities' livelihoods, the advancement of social justice, and the industry as a whole.

Developing local communities through knowledge exchange, capacity building, and community involvement is a key component of ethical herbal tea production. By offering opportunities for education and training, employers can help employees and farmers improve their knowledge and adopt sustainable farming methods. Involving local communities in decision-making processes, interacting with them, and honoring their cultural traditions all help to increase their feeling of ownership and make sure that their perspectives are heard and valued.

In order to ensure the production of ethical herbal tea, transparency and traceability in the supply chain are essential. The origin of the herbs, the farming methods used, and the social and environmental effects of the tea production process are various subjects of growing consumer interest. Businesses that place a high priority on transparency give consumers comprehensive information about their sourcing procedures, certifications, and sustainability programs, empowering them to choose ethical products and support them.

Herbal teas frequently incorporate indigenous practices and traditional knowledge. Recognizing and upholding indigenous communities' intellectual property rights and promoting the preservation of their traditional medical practices are ethical considerations. Indigenous communities can be preserved and revived by working together, involving them in the production of herbal teas, and making sure they receive fair compensation for their expertise and resources.

A wide range of values that support sustainability, social justice, transparency, and community empowerment are taken into account when producing herbal tea. The herbal tea industry can contribute to positive change by adopting sustainable farming methods, protecting biodiversity, encouraging fair trade, strengthening local communities, ensuring supply chain transparency, and honoring indigenous knowledge. As consumers, we have the ability to support businesses that share our values and prioritize herbal teas that are made from sources that are sustainable and ethically harvested. We support a more equitable and sustainable future for the environment and the communities involved in the tea business by encouraging an ethical approach to the production of herbal tea.

Supporting fair trade and eco-friendly practices

Due to their therapeutic abilities, distinctive flavors, and health advantages, herbal teas have gained popularity recently. Supporting fair trade and eco-friendly practices in the manufacturing of herbal tea has grown more important as customers become more aware of the environmental and social effects of their choices. While eco-friendly techniques place a priority on sustainability and reduce environmental harm, fair trade ensures that farmers and employees are paid fairly and treated ethically. This section will discuss the value of encouraging fair trade and environmentally friendly manufacturing methods for herbal teas, as well as the advantages these practices have for local economies and the environment.

In order to ensure that farmers and other workers who are involved in the production of herbal tea are fairly compensated for their labor, fair trade principles are based on social justice. By purchasing fair trade herbal teas, consumers help establish fair trading practices, empower farmers and workers, and enhance their standard of living. In order to assist farmers develop their abilities, embrace sustainable agricultural methods, and raise the quality of their teas, fair trade groups offer training, information, and resources. Additionally, fair trade premiums support community development initiatives that improve the general well-being of farming communities, such as the construction of schools, hospitals, or clean water programs.

Sustainable manufacturing methods for herbal tea put an emphasis on minimizing negative environmental effects. Organic farming, agroforestry, water conservation, biodiversity preservation, and waste reduction are some of these methods. Synthetic pesticides and fertilizers are not used in organic farming, protecting the water supply and soil quality. Agroforestry systems combine tea farming with tree planting, boosting soil fertility, encouraging biodiversity, and sequestering carbon. Techniques for conserving water, like effective irrigation techniques, aid in the preservation of limited water supplies. Customers can help protect ecosystems, reduce chemical pollution, and lessen the effects of climate change by purchasing herbal tea from companies that value eco-friendly methods.

In order to support fair trade and environmentally sustainable practices in the manufacture of herbal tea, ethical sourcing and transparent supply chains are essential. To ensure fair prices and working conditions, ethical sourcing entails dealing directly with farmers, cooperatives, or small-scale producers. Companies may help farmers by forming long-term partnerships that offer stability and support, allowing them to invest in sustainable practices. Customers may track the path of their tea through transparent supply chains, assuring that it was manufactured and sourced ethically. This openness covers the origin of the tea, the cultivation methods used, and any labels or certifications that attest to its moral and environmentally friendly qualities.

Beyond purely financial gains, supporting fair trade and environmentally friendly methods of producing herbal tea is important. Additionally, it promotes empowerment and community development. By including farming communities in decision-making processes and respecting their cultural traditions, fair trade organizations work closely with farming communities. This involvement promotes the preservation of indigenous knowledge and gives communities the power to reclaim control of their resources and history. Customers may support sustainable development, the reduction of poverty, and social empowerment by purchasing herbal tea from companies that value fair trade and environmentally responsible business practices.

The demand for herbal teas that are fair trade and environmentally sustainable is significantly influenced by consumer knowledge. Consumers can make moral decisions that are in line with their values by learning more about the tea brands they support. On product packaging or business websites, they can search for recognized fair trade certifications, organic labeling, and information about transparent sourcing. In order to promote local economies and lessen the carbon footprint associated with long-distance shipping, consumers can also support regional tea producers or cooperatives who place a priority on fair trade and environmentally responsible practices.

Supporting fair trade and environmentally friendly herbal tea production methods is a potent approach for consumers to help create a society that is more equitable and sustainable. Customers that choose fair trade herbal teas enable farmers and workers, enhance their livelihoods, and promote community growth. Supporting eco-friendly activities also lessens the influence on the environment, encourages biodiversity, and slows down climate change. The teas we enjoy are made in a responsible and sustainable manner due to ethical sourcing and open supply chains. Consumers can play a vital part in influencing the future of herbal tea production and bring about positive change for both people and the environment by making informed decisions and standing up for fair trade and environmentally sustainable practices.

Conclusion

Recap of the benefits and joys of crafting herbal tea blends

Making herbal tea blends is a fun and rewarding hobby that enables people to delve into the huge universe of flavors, herbs, and scents. It's essential to review the numerous benefits and pleasures that herbal tea blending offers as we approach the conclusion of our journey through this subject. The main benefits of creating herbal tea blends will be covered in this section, along with the delights that await individuals who take on this healthy and creative endeavor.

Making herbal tea blends gives you an opportunity to create flavor profiles that are unique to your tastes and requirements. Tea enthusiasts can make distinctive blends that are tailored to their taste preferences and desired medicinal effects by adding various herbs, spices, and botanicals. The choices are limitless, whether it's a calming blend for stress relief, an energizing blend for energy, or a cooling blend for hot summer days. Each cup of tea is a joyful and rewarding experience because of this customization.

Utilizing the wellness and health-promoting qualities of diverse herbs is one of the intriguing benefits of creating herbal tea blends. Various plants have particular medicinal properties, such as the ability to quiet the mind, aid with digestion, strengthen the immune system, or encourage relaxation. People can make personalized tea blends that address their particular wellness goals by mixing particular herbs. As a result, tea enthusiasts are better equipped to actively take charge of their health and include natural remedies into their everyday routines.

Making herbal tea blends includes using all of the senses and enjoying the benefits of aromatherapy. The alluring scents of herbs, flowers, and spices enhance the sense of smell and promote serenity and relaxation. A sensory experience that is both revitalizing and comforting can be experienced by preparing and enjoying tea, breathing in the calming aromas, and letting the flavors dance on the taste buds. The process of creating herbal tea blends transforms into a sensory journey that raises the spirit and provides moments of calm.

Making herbal tea blends is an artistic endeavor that enables people to express their capacity for creativity and discover their inner herbal alchemist. Tea enthusiasts can experiment with various pairings, ratios, and methods to produce blends that showcase their individual creativity because they have access to a broad variety of herbs and botanicals. The technique of herb blending allows one to experiment with flavors, colors, and textures to create visually beautiful and harmonious compositions. This form of artistic expression makes people happy and gives them a sense of success.

Making herbal tea blends encourages sustainability and builds a strong connection with nature. Tea enthusiasts can support environmentally friendly practices and help to preserve biodiversity by choosing herbs that are sustainably sourced and ingredients that are organic or locally farmed. Herbal tea blending fosters a respect for and a desire to preserve the natural world. In addition, cultivating and collecting herbs in one's own garden fosters a stronger connection with nature and promotes a sustainable way of living.

In conclusion, creating herbal tea blends is a rewarding process that has many advantages and joys that are good for the health and the soul. Blending herbal teas has many benefits, from distinctive flavor profiles to health advantages and sensory delights. The artistic expression and creative process used in creating distinctive blends promote feelings of fulfillment and success. The technique also fosters sustainability and environmental awareness by reconnecting us with nature. Let's embrace this enriching activity as we consider the advantages and pleasures of creating our own herbal tea blends and keep discovering all the possibilities the world of herbs and teas has to offer. May each cup of herbal tea we make serve as an opportunity for happiness, rest, and self-care.

Encouragement to continue exploring and experimenting

Personal growth and development require a path of exploration and experimentation with new experiences. When it comes to the realm of herbal tea, this is accurate. It is essential to urge tea enthusiasts to continue their exploration and experimentation as we draw closer to the end of this investigation. In this section, we'll explore the benefits of herbal teas, why it's crucial to keep learning about them, and how doing so helps lead a happy and meaningful life.

Herbal tea exploration and experimentation allow people to embrace their sense of adventure and curiosity. The world of herbal teas offers a limitless variety of flavors, aromas, and therapeutic characteristics waiting to be discovered, just as life offers a wide range of experiences and opportunities. Tea enthusiasts can begin on a voyage of limitless possibilities by approaching herbal tea with an open mind and a willingness to experiments with new combinations. Embracing this spirit of discovery encourages exploration in various spheres of life in addition to adding excitement and freshness to their tea experiences.

Exploring herbal teas broadens one's horizons in terms of knowledge and understanding of the natural world. Every herb has a distinct history, cultural significance, and therapeutic qualities. People who delve deeper into the realm of herbal teas might learn fascinating facts about herbs, their history, and their traditional use. This increase in knowledge boosts their enthusiasm for nature's wonders and broadens their awareness of the natural world. A person's awareness of self-care techniques and the possible advantages that herbal teas may provide for general well-being is also increased by learning about new herbs and their qualities.

Herbal tea experimentation is a creative outlet that promotes self-expression. Blending various herbs, spices, and botanicals is an art form that encourages people to let their creativity run wild and develop distinctive flavor profiles. It inspires people to use their creative abilities and combine herbs in fresh ways. Tea enthusiasts can create their own distinctive blends through this procedure that represent their own tastes, preferences, and aspirations. Through this creative outlet, people can express their individual personalities and styles and feel accomplished.

Herbal tea exploration and experimentation foster mindfulness and promote the development of meaningful rituals. Making and enjoying a cup of herbal tea turns into a ritualistic activity that encourages people to take their time, be in the present, and use all of their senses. It offers an opportunity to detach from the busyness of everyday life and find comfort in the simple pleasure of taking a cup of tea. People can develop their mindfulness practices and develop rituals that are nourishing to their mind, body, and soul by continuing to learn about herbal teas.

Herbal tea exploration and experimentation provide opportunities to interact with a thriving tea enthusiast community. People can share their experiences, gain knowledge from others, and exchange ideas through internet forums, tea tastings, and regional tea events. By participating in a group of people who share your interests, you can develop a sense of community and foster an encouraging atmosphere for ongoing learning and exploration. It offers a forum for exchanging knowledge, anecdotes, and recipes as well as for inspiring and being inspired by others on their own tea adventures.

In conclusion, an advice to keep learning and experimenting about herbal teas is a call to embrace curiosity, increase knowledge, unleash creativity, cultivate awareness, and establish connections with other tea enthusiasts. Individuals can start on a journey of self-discovery, personal expression, and wellness by delving further into the world of herbal teas. Let us embrace the delight of discovery as we travel this path, keep an open mind, and savor the herbal teas' numerous variety of flavors and aromas. May the warmth and excitement that come from discovering the virtually limitless possibilities that the world of herbal teas offers overflow into our cups.

Final thoughts and closing remarks

As this exploration into the world of herbal teas comes to an end, it is time to consider the insights learned, the stories shared, and the significant influence herbal teas can have on our lives. We will discuss our final ideas and concluding observations in this section, summarizing the main lessons learned from our experience and leaving you feeling inspired and grateful for the world of herbal teas.

We have seen the tremendous power of herbal teas, one of nature's many gifts, throughout our exploration. Every herb, from the delicate chamomile petals to the sturdy peppermint leaves, has a distinct fragrance that can be used therapeutically and to improve our well-being. It serves as a reminder of how closely related nature and humanity are, as well as the knowledge that nature offers. We may draw on this age-old knowledge and let nature sooth our bodies, minds, and spirits by incorporating herbal teas.

Herbal teas provide a transformative journey toward well-being and self-care. It motivates us to take a moment, think, and give attention to our well-being. Herbal teas offer a delicate yet effective self-care aid, from the calming effects of lavender to the energizing effects of ginger. Herbal teas help us take care of our bodies, increase mindfulness, and create peaceful moments in a frequently chaotic environment. Herbal teas' journey serves as a constant reminder to put self-care first and pay attention to our physical, emotional, and spiritual needs.

The discovery of a broad tapestry of flavors and scents is one of the biggest pleasures of learning about herbal teas. Herbal teas provide a limitless variety of sensory experiences, ranging from earthy and calming herbal blends to the vibrant and energizing flavors of fruit infusions. Each sip invites us to go on a sensory journey that awakens our taste buds and arouses our senses. Exploring flavors and aromas in herbal teas opens up a whole new world of culinary creativity and the chance to create unique, delectable beverages.

Teas made from herbs have a remarkable capacity to unite people, forge bonds, and promote a sense of community. The ritual of tea ignites conversations, strengthens bonds, and fosters a sense of belonging, whether it's drinking a cup of tea with loved ones, taking part in tea ceremonies, or attending events related to tea. We find a bond that crosses boundaries and unites people from many origins and cultures through our mutual appreciation of herbal teas. The herbal tea industry is a potent connector, serving as a reminder of our connected humanity and the bonds we establish through shared experiences.

It's important to keep in mind that learning about the world of herbal teas is a lifelong journey as we come to the end of this exploration. There are always new herbs to discover, unique combinations to develop, and novel viewpoints to acquire. The more we learn about the world of herbal teas, the bigger and more complex it seems to be. It is a journey that inspires us to maintain our curiosity, mental flexibility, and openness to new possibilities. With every new cup of tea, we set off on an adventure that fosters our development, broadens our perspectives, and encourages us to keep discovering the wonders of nature's therapeutic gifts.

In conclusion, learning about herbal teas is a rewarding and transformational experience. It includes the power of nature, the value of taking care of oneself, the fun of sensory encounters, the links of community, and the limitless opportunities for learning. Let's carry the knowledge we've received and the adventures we've had in our hearts as we conclude this chapter. Let's continue to appreciate herbal teas' therapeutic and nourishing properties, cultivate moments of peace and connection, and nourish ourselves and others by simply sharing a cup of tea. May this journey serve as a daily reminder to take it easy, appreciate the present moment, and find comfort in nature's offerings. Cheers to the wonderful world of herbal teas and the limitless opportunities it provides for a happy and fulfilling life.

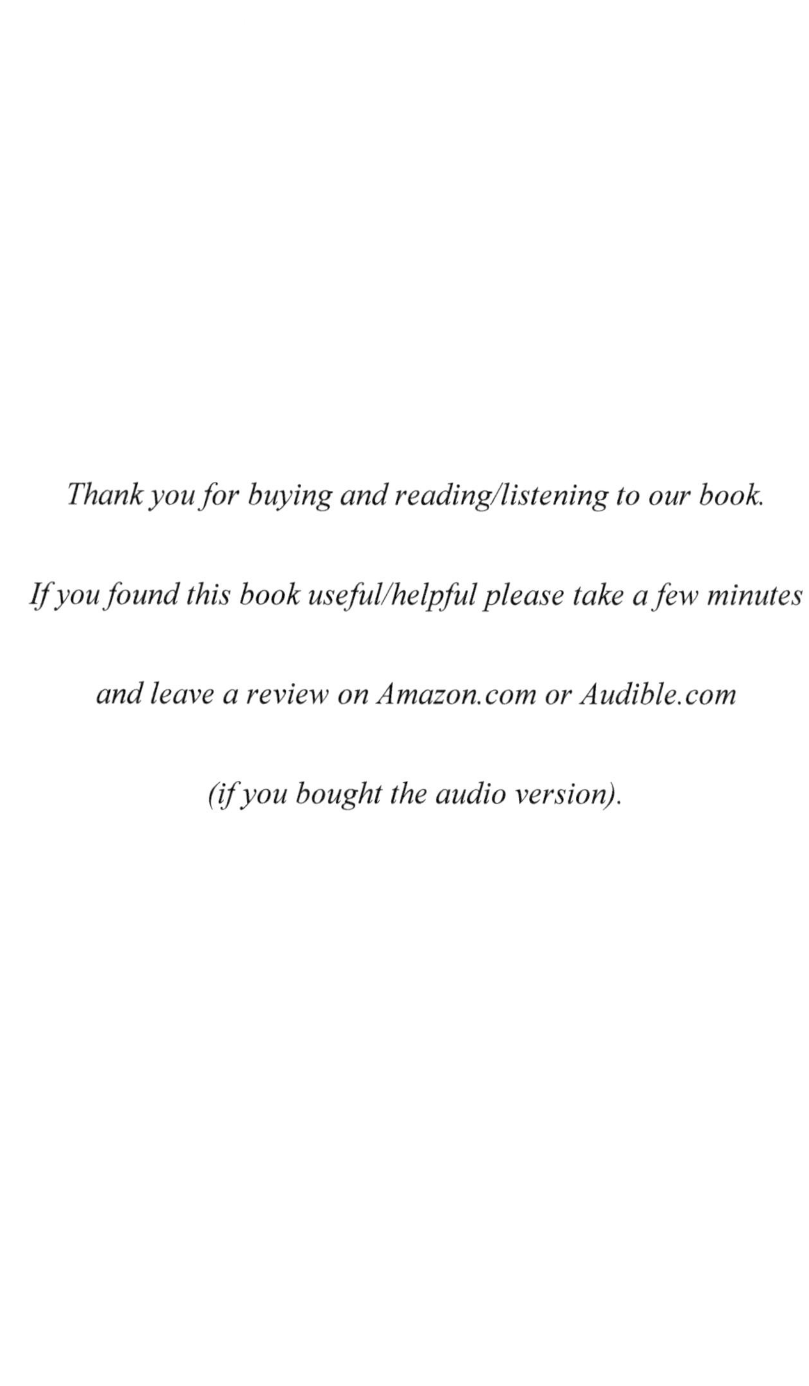

Thank you for buying and reading/listening to our book.

If you found this book useful/helpful please take a few minutes

and leave a review on Amazon.com or Audible.com

(if you bought the audio version).